THE PARALLEL
WESTMINSTER SHORTER CATECHISM
HANDBOOK

THE PARALLEL
WESTMINSTER SHORTER CATECHISM
HANDBOOK

PARAPHRASED AND EDITED BY
CAROLINE WEERSTRA

Common Life Press
Schenectady, New York
www.commonlifepress.com

Published by Common Life Press, Schenectady, New York. 2012.

ISBN-13: 978-0983724940

Scripture taken from the New King James Version. Copyright © 1982 by Thomas Nelson, Inc. Used by permission. All rights reserved.

Copyright © 2012 by Caroline Weerstra. All rights reserved. No part of this publication may be reproduced or transmitted by electronic, photocopy, or other means without prior written permission of the publisher.

INTRODUCTION

"The Devil give you colic in your stomach, false thief! Do you dare say the mass in my ear?"

Jenny Geddes, a poor Scottish woman in 1637, spoke these words, and she punctuated them by flinging a stool at the head of a minister. Although no one would have anticipated it at the time, this unlikely action marked the beginning of a movement which eventually led to the writing of the Westminster Confession of Faith, as well as the Shorter Catechism and Larger Catechism.

By the time Jenny Geddes let fly her stool, the Reformation was already well-established in the British Isles. In England, Henry VIII had deposed the authority of the pope and replaced Catholicism with the Church of England, over which he ruled.

Many people, however, resented the corruption in the newly established state church and recognized that the liturgical rituals differed very little from Catholicism. These reformers were dubbed "Puritans" because of their insistence upon purification of both church and society.

In Scotland, John Knox and others had persuaded the Scottish Parliament to abandon Catholicism in 1560 and to establish the Reformed faith in the new Church of Scotland.

Charles I ascended to the throne in 1625 with a dream of uniting England and Scotland into a single kingdom under his personal rule. In order to avoid challenges to his authority, he refused to convene an English Parliament. Charles also supported High Anglicanism as the state church, and he sought to implement it in all English churches. When Puritans protested the Arminian theology and Catholic ritual, Charles ordered them arrested.

Tensions continued to mount as Charles drew up plans to introduce High Anglican worship in Scotland. He ordered a new Anglican *Book of Common Prayer* to be used in the Church of Scotland.

On Sunday, June 23, 1637, the Dean of Edinburgh, James Hannay, stood up at St. Giles' Cathedral to read from the new liturgy. Jenny Geddes, a market woman seated on a small stool, expressed the outrage of the whole community as she flung her chair at his head and exclaimed, "Do you dare say the mass in my ear?"

A riot broke out. Even after the angry mob had been expelled from the church, they continued to beat on the door and throw rocks at the windows.

Scotland demanded the withdrawal of the Anglican liturgy, but King Charles refused. In a short period of time, both England and Scotland had plunged into war. The Covenanters (a Scottish Presbyterian movement) raised an army and defeated Charles, forcing him to withdraw. Charles (in desperate need of money to hold on to his claim to the Scottish throne) finally convened Parliament in order to raise funds. By this time, however, Parliament had turned against him. Soon those on the side of Parliament and those on the side of the king were taking up arms against each other. Civil war had broken out in England.

The English Parliament sought an alliance with the Scottish Covenanters in order to overthrow King Charles. The Covenanters agreed, but stipulated that the new government must hold to Reformed theology as the state church.

On October 12, 1643, the Westminster divines, a group of 121 clergymen, began work on a set of standards for the reformation of the state church in England. The resulting documents were the Westminster Confession of Faith and the Larger and Shorter Catechisms. These works were presented to Parliament in 1648, the same year that King Charles was finally overthrown. He was convicted of treason and executed on January 30, 1649.

The victory for the Puritans was short-lived. In 1660, Charles II (the son of Charles I) restored the monarchy and reinstated the Church of England. The Westminster Confession of Faith was officially revoked.

Although no longer a political document, the Westminster Confession and the Catechisms continued to gather momentum in Reformed churches throughout the English-speaking world. As a summary of Scriptural teaching, these documents are unrivaled. Even today, more than 350 years after their completion, they still form the basis of Reformed doctrine. Even many non-Reformed churches use the Confession and Catechisms to introduce people to Scriptural teaching.

The Westminster Shorter Catechism is composed of 107 brief questions and answers divided into two main parts:

- Questions 1-38: What is God?
- Questions 39-107: What does God require of us?

The Westminster Shorter Catechism was composed primarily as a tool for instructing children and new converts. The Scripture-based theology within the

Westminster standards is timeless, and it applies to us today as much as it did when it was written. However, language changes over the course of many years, and modern churches often find that children, new converts, and even average parishioners have considerable difficulty understanding the antiquated language used in the Catechism.

In this handbook, the original Shorter Catechism is set alongside a modern paraphrase, in order to assist with comprehension. Scripture proofs are displayed below each question and answer to assist with more in-depth study.

In one sense, the Westminster Shorter Catechism is nothing new. Not only is it hundreds of years old, but every line is based upon Christian doctrines established in Scripture and taught in the Church for generations. The strength of the Shorter Catechism lies in its systematic organization, its concise but thorough discussion of basic biblical doctrine, and its beautiful expression of timeless Christian truths. It teaches us about the attributes of God and the redemption found in Christ. It reminds us that our main purpose in life is to glorify God and to enjoy Him forever.

QUESTION 1

ORIGINAL

Q. 1. What is the chief end of man?

A. Man's chief end is to glorify God, and to enjoy him forever.

MODERN

Q. 1. What is the main purpose of all people?

A. The main purpose of all people is to honor God and to enjoy Him forever.

> **PROOF TEXTS**
>
> **I Corinthians 10:31** Therefore, whether you eat or drink, or whatever you do, do all to the glory of God.
>
> **Romans 11:36** For of Him and through Him and to Him are all things, to whom be glory forever. Amen.
>
> **Psalm 73:25-28** Whom have I in heaven but You? And there is none upon earth that I desire besides You. My flesh and my heart fail; but God is the strength of my heart and my portion forever. For indeed, those who are far from You shall perish; You have destroyed all those who desert You for harlotry. But it is good for me to draw near to God; I have put my trust in the Lord GOD, that I may declare all Your works.

QUESTION 2

ORIGINAL

Q. 2. What rule hath God given to direct us how we may glorify and enjoy him?

A. The Word of God, which is contained in the Scriptures of the Old and New Testaments, is the only rule to direct us how we may glorify and enjoy him.

MODERN

Q. 2. What has God given to instruct us regarding the proper way to honor and enjoy Him?

A. The Word of God (which is contained in the Bible in both the Old Testament and the New Testament) is the only set of instructions given by God to explain how we may honor and enjoy Him.

PROOF TEXTS
II Timothy 3:16 All Scripture is given by inspiration of God, and is profitable for doctrine, for reproof, for correction, for instruction in righteousness.
Ephesians 2:20 having been built on the foundation of the apostles and prophets, Jesus Christ Himself being the chief cornerstone
I John 1:3-4 That which we have seen and heard we declare to you, that you also may have fellowship with us; and truly our fellowship is with the Father and with His Son Jesus Christ. And these things we write to you that your joy may be full.

QUESTION 3

ORIGINAL

Q. 3. What do the Scriptures principally teach?

A. The Scriptures principally teach what man is to believe concerning God, and what duty God requires of man.

MODERN

Q. 3. What does the Bible primarily teach us?

A. The Bible primarily teaches us what we must believe about God and how we should obey Him.

PROOF TEXTS

II Timothy 1:13 Hold fast the pattern of sound words which you have heard from me, in faith and love which are in Christ Jesus.

II Timothy 3:16 All Scripture is given by inspiration of God, and is profitable for doctrine, for reproof, for correction, for instruction in righteousness.

QUESTION 4

ORIGINAL

Q. 4. What is God?

A. God is a Spirit, infinite, eternal, and unchangeable, in his being, wisdom, power, holiness, justice, goodness, and truth.

MODERN

Q. 4. What is God?

A. God does not have a body. He is limitless and eternal. He never changes. His characteristics—wisdom, power, holiness, justice, goodness, and truth—are also limitless, eternal, and unchanging.

PROOF TEXTS

John 4:24 God is Spirit, and those who worship Him must worship in spirit and truth.

Job 11:7-9 Can you search out the deep things of God? Can you find out the limits of the Almighty? They are higher than heaven— what can you do? Deeper than Sheol— what can you know? Their measure is longer than the earth and broader than the sea.

Psalm 90:2 Before the mountains were brought forth, or ever You had formed the earth and the world, even from everlasting to everlasting, You are God.

James 1:17 Every good gift and every perfect gift is from above, and comes down from the Father of lights, with whom there is no variation or shadow of turning.

Exodus 3:14 And God said to Moses, "I AM WHO I AM." And He said, "Thus you shall say to the children of Israel, 'I AM has sent me to you.'"

Psalm 147:5 Great is our Lord, and mighty in power; His understanding is infinite.

Revelation 4:8 The four living creatures, each having six wings, were full of eyes around and within. And they do not rest day or night, saying: "Holy, holy, holy, Lord God Almighty, who was and is and is to come!"

Revelation 15:4 Who shall not fear You, O Lord, and glorify Your name? For You alone are holy. For all nations shall come and worship before You, for Your judgments have been manifested.

Exodus 34:6-7 And the LORD passed before him and proclaimed, "The LORD, the LORD God, merciful and gracious, longsuffering, and abounding in goodness and truth, keeping mercy for thousands, forgiving iniquity and transgression and sin, by no means clearing the guilty, visiting the iniquity of the fathers upon the children and the children's children to the third and the fourth generation."

QUESTION 5

ORIGINAL

Q. 5. Are there more Gods than one?

A. There is but one only, the living and true God.

MODERN

Q. 5. How many Gods exist?

A. There is only one God—the living and true God.

PROOF TEXTS
Deuteronomy 6:4 Hear, O Israel: The LORD our God, the LORD is one!

QUESTION 6

ORIGINAL

Q. 6. How many persons are there in the Godhead?

A. There are three persons in the Godhead: the Father, the Son, and the Holy Ghost; and these three are one God, the same in substance, equal in power and glory.

MODERN

Q. 6. How many Persons are there in God?

A. There are three: the Father, the Son, and the Holy Spirit. These three are one God. They are the same in substance, and They are equal in power and glory.

PROOF TEXTS
I John 5:7 For there are three that bear witness in heaven: the Father, the Word, and the Holy Spirit; and these three are one.
Matthew 28:19 Go therefore and make disciples of all the nations, baptizing them in the name of the Father and of the Son and of the Holy Spirit.

QUESTION 7

ORIGINAL

Q. 7. What are the decrees of God?

A. The decrees of God are his eternal purpose, according to the counsel of his will, whereby, for his own glory, he hath foreordained whatsoever comes to pass.

MODERN

Q. 7. What are God's decrees?

A. God's decrees are His eternal plan, which depends entirely upon His will. Before anything happens, He has already planned it for His own glory.

PROOF TEXTS
Ephesians 1:4 just as He chose us in Him before the foundation of the world, that we should be holy and without blame before Him in love
Ephesians 1:11 In Him also we have obtained an inheritance, being predestined according to the purpose of Him who works all things according to the counsel of His will.
Romans 9:22-23 What if God, wanting to show His wrath and to make His power known, endured with much longsuffering the vessels of wrath prepared for destruction, and that He might make known the riches of His glory on the vessels of mercy, which He had prepared beforehand for glory.

QUESTION 8

ORIGINAL

Q. 8. How doth God execute his decrees?

A. God executeth his decrees in the works of creation and providence.

MODERN

Q. 8. How does God carry out His decrees?

A. God carries out His decrees through His works of creation and providence.

QUESTION 9

ORIGINAL

Q. 9. What is the work of creation?

A. The work of creation is, God's making all things of nothing, by the word of his power, in the space of six days, and all very good.

MODERN

Q. 9. What is God's work of creation?

A. Through His powerful Word, God made everything out of nothing. He accomplished this work within six days, and everything He created was very good.

PROOF TEXTS
Genesis 1:1 In the beginning God created the heavens and the earth.
Hebrews 11:3 By faith we understand that the worlds were framed by the word of God, so that the things which are seen were not made of things which are visible.

QUESTION 10

ORIGINAL

Q. 10. How did God create man?

A. God created man male and female, after his own image, in knowledge, righteousness, and holiness, with dominion over the creatures.

MODERN

Q. 10. How did God create man and woman?

A. God created man and woman to look like Himself. Men and women reflect God in their knowledge, righteousness, holiness, and authority over other creatures.

> **PROOF TEXTS**
>
> **Genesis 1:26-28** Then God said, "Let Us make man in Our image, according to Our likeness; let them have dominion over the fish of the sea, over the birds of the air, and over the cattle, over all the earth and over every creeping thing that creeps on the earth." So God created man in His own image; in the image of God He created him; male and female He created them. Then God blessed them, and God said to them, "Be fruitful and multiply; fill the earth and subdue it; have dominion over the fish of the sea, over the birds of the air, and over every living thing that moves on the earth."
>
> **Colossians 3:10** and have put on the new man who is renewed in knowledge according to the image of Him who created him
>
> **Ephesians 4:24** and that you put on the new man which was created according to God, in true righteousness and holiness

QUESTION 11

ORIGINAL

Q. 11. What are God's works of providence?

A. God's works of providence are, his most holy, wise, and powerful preserving and governing all his creatures, and all their actions.

MODERN

Q. 11. What are God's works of providence?

A. God's works of providence are the things He does in order to maintain and oversee His creatures and everything they do. His providence is always holy, wise, and powerful.

> **PROOF TEXTS**
>
> **Psalm 145:17** The Lord is righteous in all His ways, gracious in all His works.
>
> **Psalm 104:24** O LORD, how manifold are Your works! In wisdom You have made them all. The earth is full of Your possessions.
>
> **Isaiah 28:29** This also comes from the LORD of hosts, who is wonderful in counsel and excellent in guidance.
>
> **Hebrews 1:3** who being the brightness of His glory and the express image of His person, and upholding all things by the word of His power, when He had by Himself purged our sins, sat down at the right hand of the Majesty on high
>
> **Psalm 103:19** The LORD has established His throne in heaven, and His kingdom rules over all.

QUESTION 12

ORIGINAL

Q. 12. What special act of providence did God exercise towards man in the estate wherein he was created?

A. When God had created man, he entered into a covenant of life with him, upon condition of perfect obedience; forbidding him to eat of the tree of the knowledge of good and evil, upon the pain of death.

MODERN

Q. 12. What did God do for the man he had created (before the Fall) as a special act of His providence?

A. When God created Adam, He entered into a contract of life with him. The contract required that mankind must obey God's commandments perfectly. The man was instructed not to eat the fruit from the tree of the knowledge of good and evil, and he was warned that he would die if he disobeyed.

PROOF TEXTS

Galatians 3:12 Yet the law is not of faith, but *"the man who does them shall live by them."*

Genesis 2:17 but of the tree of the knowledge of good and evil you shall not eat, for in the day that you eat of it you shall surely die

QUESTION 13

ORIGINAL

Q. 13. Did our first parents continue in the estate wherein they were created?

A. Our first parents, being left to the freedom of their own will, fell from the estate wherein they were created, by sinning against God.

MODERN

Q. 13. Did the first man and woman (our ancestors) continue in the state of perfection in which God had made them?

A. The first man and woman fell from their state of perfection. They were able to choose whether to obey God or disobey Him. They sinned against God through their own bad choices.

> **PROOF TEXTS**
>
> **Genesis 3:6-8** So when the woman saw that the tree was good for food, that it was pleasant to the eyes, and a tree desirable to make one wise, she took of its fruit and ate. She also gave to her husband with her, and he ate. Then the eyes of both of them were opened, and they knew that they were naked; and they sewed fig leaves together and made themselves coverings. And they heard the sound of the LORD God walking in the garden in the cool of the day, and Adam and his wife hid themselves from the presence of the LORD God among the trees of the garden.
>
> **Ecclesiastes 7:29** Truly, this only I have found: that God made man upright, but they have sought out many schemes.

QUESTION 14

ORIGINAL

Q. 14. What is sin?

A. Sin is any want of conformity unto, or transgression of, the law of God.

MODERN

Q. 14. What is sin?

A. Sin is any failure to obey the law of God or any act of rebellion against the law of God.

PROOF TEXTS
I John 3:4 Whoever commits sin also commits lawlessness, and sin is lawlessness.

QUESTION 15

ORIGINAL

Q. 15. What was the sin whereby our first parents fell from the estate wherein they were created?

A. The sin whereby our first parents fell from the estate wherein they were created, was their eating the forbidden fruit.

MODERN

Q. 15. What sin led to the fall of the first man and woman from the state of perfection in which God had created them?

A. The first man and woman fell from the state of perfection by eating the fruit which God had forbidden them to eat.

PROOF TEXTS
Genesis 3:6 So when the woman saw that the tree was good for food, that it was pleasant to the eyes, and a tree desirable to make one wise, she took of its fruit and ate. She also gave to her husband with her, and he ate.

QUESTION 16

ORIGINAL

Q. 16. Did all mankind fall in Adam's first transgression?

A. The covenant being made with Adam, not only for himself, but for his posterity; all mankind, descending from him by ordinary generation, sinned in him, and fell with him, in his first transgression.

MODERN

Q. 16. Did all mankind fall when Adam sinned?

A. God's contract was made with Adam, but it was not only for him. All of Adam's children, grandchildren, and further descendants were included in the contract. Therefore, all humans (born in the ordinary manner) sinned when Adam sinned. All mankind fell with Adam.

PROOF TEXTS
Romans 5:12 Therefore, just as through one man sin entered the world, and death through sin, and thus death spread to all men, because all sinned.
I Corinthians 15:21-22 For since by man came death, by Man also came the resurrection of the dead. For as in Adam all die, even so in Christ all shall be made alive.

QUESTION 17

ORIGINAL

Q. 17. Into what estate did the fall bring mankind?

A. The fall brought mankind into an estate of sin and misery.

MODERN

Q. 17. What condition did the Fall bring upon all mankind?

A. The Fall brought sin and misery on all people.

PROOF TEXTS
Romans 5:12 Therefore, just as through one man sin entered the world, and death through sin, and thus death spread to all men, because all sinned.

QUESTION 18

ORIGINAL

Q. 18. Wherein consists the sinfulness of that estate whereinto man fell?

A. The sinfulness of that estate whereinto man fell, consists in the guilt of Adam's first sin, the want of original righteousness, and the corruption of his whole nature, which is commonly called Original Sin; together with all actual transgressions which proceed from it.

MODERN

Q. 18. How is the fallen condition of mankind sinful?

A. The fallen condition of mankind includes the guilt of Adam's first sin. Since mankind has fallen, all humans are corrupt, lacking fundamental righteousness in their nature. This is generally referred to as *original sin*. Additionally, everyone commits actual sins as a result of their sinful nature.

PROOF TEXTS
Romans 5:12 Therefore, just as through one man sin entered the world, and death through sin, and thus death spread to all men, because all sinned.
Romans 5:19 For as by one man's disobedience many were made sinners, so also by one Man's obedience many will be made righteous.

Romans 5:10-20 For if when we were enemies we were reconciled to God through the death of His Son, much more, having been reconciled, we shall be saved by His life. And not only that, but we also rejoice in God through our Lord Jesus Christ, through whom we have now received the reconciliation. Therefore, just as through one man sin entered the world, and death through sin, and thus death spread to all men, because all sinned— (For until the law sin was in the world, but sin is not imputed when there is no law. Nevertheless death reigned from Adam to Moses, even over those who had not sinned according to the likeness of the transgression of Adam, who is a type of Him who was to come. But the free gift is not like the offense. For if by the one man's offense many died, much more the grace of God and the gift by the grace of the one Man, Jesus Christ, abounded to many. And the gift is not like that which came through the one who sinned. For the judgment which came from one offense resulted in condemnation, but the free gift which came from many offenses resulted in justification. For if by the one man's offense death reigned through the one, much more those who receive abundance of grace and of the gift of righteousness will reign in life through the One, Jesus Christ.) Therefore, as through one man's offense judgment came to all men, resulting in condemnation, even so through one Man's righteous act the free gift came to all men, resulting in justification of life. For as by one man's disobedience many were made sinners, so also by one Man's obedience many will be made righteous. Moreover the law entered that the offense might abound. But where sin abounded, grace abounded much more.

James 1:14-15 But each one is tempted when he is drawn away by his own desires and enticed. Then, when desire has conceived, it gives birth to sin; and sin, when it is full-grown, brings forth death.

Matthew 15:19 For out of the heart proceed evil thoughts, murders, adulteries, fornications, thefts, false witness, blasphemies.

QUESTION 19

ORIGINAL

Q. 19. What is the misery of that estate whereinto man fell?

A. All mankind by their fall lost communion with God, are under his wrath and curse, and so made liable to all miseries in this life, to death itself, and to the pains of hell for ever.

MODERN

Q. 19. What misery did the Fall bring on mankind?

A. Because of the Fall, everyone lost fellowship with God and came under God's anger and curse. All humankind is subject to suffering in life and, ultimately, to death and hell.

> **PROOF TEXTS**
>
> **Genesis 3:24** So He drove out the man; and He placed cherubim at the east of the garden of Eden, and a flaming sword which turned every way, to guard the way to the tree of life.
>
> **Ephesians 2:2-3** in which you once walked according to the course of this world, according to the prince of the power of the air, the spirit who now works in the sons of disobedience, among whom also we all once conducted ourselves in the lusts of our flesh, fulfilling the desires of the flesh and of the mind, and were by nature children of wrath, just as the others.

QUESTION 20

ORIGINAL

Q. 20. Did God leave all mankind to perish in the estate of sin and misery?

A. God having, out of his mere good pleasure, from all eternity, elected some to everlasting life, did enter into a covenant of grace, to deliver them out of the estate of sin and misery, and to bring them into an estate of salvation by a Redeemer.

MODERN

Q. 20. Did God leave all mankind to die in their sin and misery?

A. It pleased God to choose certain people (His elect) for eternal life. He entered into a contract of grace to save them from their sin and misery. He brought them salvation by a Redeemer.

PROOF TEXTS
Ephesians 1:4 just as He chose us in Him before the foundation of the world, that we should be holy and without blame before Him in love
Romans 3:20-23 Therefore by the deeds of the law no flesh will be justified in His sight, for by the law is the knowledge of sin. But now the righteousness of God apart from the law is revealed, being witnessed by the Law and the Prophets, even the righteousness of God, through faith in Jesus Christ, to all and on all who believe. For there is no difference; for all have sinned and fall short of the glory of God.

QUESTION 21

ORIGINAL

Q. 21. Who is the Redeemer of God's elect?

A. The only Redeemer of God's elect is the Lord Jesus Christ, who, being the eternal Son of God, became man, and so was, and continueth to be, God and man in two distinct natures, and one person, for ever.

MODERN

Q. 21. Who is the Redeemer of God's elect?

A. The only Redeemer of God's elect is the Lord Jesus Christ. He is the eternal Son of God, and yet He became man—both God and man, in two distinct natures but one Person. He remains both God and man today, and He will continue so forever.

PROOF TEXTS

I Timothy 2:5-6 For there is one God and one Mediator between God and men, the Man Christ Jesus, who gave Himself a ransom for all, to be testified in due time.

John 1:14 And the Word became flesh and dwelt among us, and we beheld His glory, the glory as of the only begotten of the Father, full of grace and truth.

Luke 1:35 And the angel answered and said to her, "The Holy Spirit will come upon you, and the power of the Highest will overshadow you; therefore, also, that Holy One who is to be born will be called the Son of God.

QUESTION 22

ORIGINAL

Q. 22. How did Christ, being the Son of God, become man?

A. Christ, the Son of God, became man, by taking to himself a true body, and a reasonable soul, being conceived by the power of the Holy Ghost, in the womb of the Virgin Mary, and born of her, yet without sin.

MODERN

Q. 22. How did Christ (the Son of God) become man?

A. Christ, the Son of God, became man by taking on a real body and a rational soul. He was conceived by the power of the Holy Spirit in the womb of the Virgin Mary. He had a human birth, yet without sin.

> **PROOF TEXTS**
>
> **Hebrews 10:5** Therefore, when He came into the world, He said: *"Sacrifice and offering You did not desire, but a body You have prepared for Me."*
>
> **Galatians 4:4** But when the fullness of the time had come, God sent forth His Son, born of a woman, born under the law.
>
> **Hebrews 4:15** For we do not have a High Priest who cannot sympathize with our weaknesses, but was in all points tempted as we are, yet without sin.

QUESTION 23

ORIGINAL

Q. 23. What offices doth Christ execute as our Redeemer?

A. Christ, as our Redeemer, executeth the offices of a prophet, of a priest, and of a king, both in his estate of humiliation and exaltation.

MODERN

Q. 23. What tasks does Christ carry out as our Redeemer?

A. As our Redeemer, Christ carries out the roles of a prophet, a priest, and a king. He has fulfilled these tasks both in His condition of humiliation and in His condition of exaltation.

> **PROOF TEXTS**
>
> **Acts 3:21-22** whom heaven must receive until the times of restoration of all things, which God has spoken by the mouth of all His holy prophets since the world began. For Moses truly said to the fathers, *'The LORD your God will raise up for you a Prophet like me from your brethren. Him you shall hear in all things, whatever He says to you.*
>
> **Hebrews 5:5-6** So also Christ did not glorify Himself to become High Priest, but it was He who said to Him: *"You are My Son, today I have begotten You."* As He also says in another place: *"You are a priest forever according to the order of Melchizedek."*
>
> **Isaiah 9:6-7** For unto us a Child is born, unto us a Son is given; and the government will be upon His shoulder. And His

name will be called Wonderful, Counselor, Mighty God, Everlasting Father, Prince of Peace. Of the increase of His government and peace there will be no end, upon the throne of David and over His kingdom, to order it and establish it with judgment and justice from that time forward, even forever. The zeal of the Lord of hosts will perform this.

QUESTION 24

ORIGINAL

Q. 24. How doth Christ execute the office of a prophet?

A. Christ executeth the office of a prophet, in revealing to us, by his word and Spirit, the will of God for our salvation.

MODERN

Q. 24. How does Christ fulfill the role of a prophet?

A. By His Word and Spirit, Christ reveals to us the will of God for our salvation. In this sense, He is our prophet.

> **PROOF TEXTS**
>
> **I Peter 1:10-12** Of this salvation the prophets have inquired and searched carefully, who prophesied of the grace that would come to you, searching what, or what manner of time, the Spirit of Christ who was in them was indicating when He testified beforehand the sufferings of Christ and the glories that would follow. To them it was revealed that, not to themselves, but to us they were ministering the things which now have been reported to you through those who have preached the gospel to you by the Holy Spirit sent from heaven—things which angels desire to look into.
>
> **John 15:15** No longer do I call you servants, for a servant does not know what his master is doing; but I have called you friends, for all things that I heard from My Father I have made known to you.

QUESTION 25

ORIGINAL

Q. 25. How doth Christ execute the office of a priest?

A. Christ executeth the office of a priest, in his once offering up of himself a sacrifice to satisfy divine justice, and reconcile us to God; and in making continual intercession for us.

MODERN

Q. 25. How does Christ fulfill the role of a priest?

A. Christ offered Himself as a sacrifice—not continually, but only once. By this sacrifice, He satisfied the requirements of God's justice and reconciled us to God. Today, Christ continues to intercede for us. In all these things, Christ is our priest.

PROOF TEXTS

Hebrews 9:14 how much more shall the blood of Christ, who through the eternal Spirit offered Himself without spot to God, cleanse your conscience from dead works to serve the living God?

Hebrews 9:28 so Christ was offered once to bear the sins of many. To those who eagerly wait for Him He will appear a second time, apart from sin, for salvation.

Hebrews 7:24-25 But He, because He continues forever, has an unchangeable priesthood. Therefore He is also able to save to the uttermost those who come to God through Him, since He always lives to make intercession for them.

QUESTION 26

ORIGINAL

Q. 26. How doth Christ execute the office of a king?

A. Christ executeth the office of a king, in subduing us to himself, in ruling and defending us, and in restraining and conquering all his and our enemies.

MODERN

Q. 26. How does Christ fulfill the role of a king?

A. Christ makes us to be His followers. He rules over us and defends us. He holds back and conquers all His enemies and our enemies. In all these things, Christ is our king.

> **PROOF TEXTS**
>
> **Isaiah 32:1-2** Behold, a king will reign in righteousness, and princes will rule with justice. A man will be as a hiding place from the wind, and a cover from the tempest, as rivers of water in a dry place, as the shadow of a great rock in a weary land.
>
> **I Corinthians 15:25** For He must reign till He has put all enemies under His feet.
>
> **Psalm 110:1-2** The LORD said to my Lord, "Sit at My right hand, till I make Your enemies Your footstool." The LORD shall send the rod of Your strength out of Zion. Rule in the midst of Your enemies!

QUESTION 27

ORIGINAL

Q. 27. Wherein did Christ's humiliation consist?

A. Christ's humiliation consisted in his being born, and that in a low condition, made under the law, undergoing the miseries of this life, the wrath of God, and the cursed death of the cross; in being buried, and continuing under the power of death for a time.

MODERN

Q. 27. What do we mean when we talk about Christ's humiliation?

A. Christ was born in a lowly condition. He lived under the law, and He suffered all the miseries of human life and the curse of God. He died a tormented death on the cross. He was buried, and He continued under the power of death for a while. This is what we mean when we speak of Christ's humiliation.

PROOF TEXTS

Luke 2:7 And she brought forth her firstborn Son, and wrapped Him in swaddling cloths, and laid Him in a manger, because there was no room for them in the inn.

Galatians 4:4 But when the fullness of the time had come, God sent forth His Son, born of a woman, born under the law.

Hebrews 12:2-3 looking unto Jesus, the author and finisher of our faith, who for the joy that was set before Him endured the cross, despising the shame, and has sat down at the right hand of the throne of God. For consider Him who endured such hostility from sinners against Himself, lest you become weary and discouraged in your souls.

Luke 22:44 And being in agony, He prayed more earnestly. Then His sweat became like great drops of blood falling down to the ground.

Matthew 27:46 And about the ninth hour Jesus cried out with a loud voice, saying, "Eli, Eli, lama sabachthani?" that is, *"My God, My God, why have You forsaken Me?"*

Philippians 2:8 And being found in appearance as a man, He humbled Himself and became obedient to the point of death, even the death of the cross.

I Corinthians 15:3-4 For I delivered to you first of all that which I also received: that Christ died for our sins according to the Scriptures, and that He was buried, and that He rose again the third day according to the Scriptures.

Acts 2:24-27 whom God raised up, having loosed the pains of death, because it was not possible that He should be held by it. For David says concerning Him: *'I foresaw the LORD always before my face, for He is at my right hand, that I may not be shaken. Therefore my heart rejoiced, and my tongue was glad; moreover my flesh also will rest in hope. For You will not leave my soul in Hades, nor will You allow Your Holy One to see corruption.'*

QUESTION 28

ORIGINAL

Q. 28. Wherein consisteth Christ's exaltation?

A. Christ's exaltation consisteth in his rising again from the dead on the third day, in ascending up into heaven, in sitting at the right hand of God the Father, and in coming to judge the world at the last day.

MODERN

Q. 28. What do we mean when we talk about Christ's exaltation?

A. Christ rose from the dead on the third day. He ascended into heaven and sat down at the right hand of God the Father. On the last day, He will return to judge the world. This is what we mean when we speak of Christ's exaltation.

PROOF TEXTS

I Corinthians 15:4 and that He was buried, and that He rose again the third day according to the Scriptures

Mark 16:19 So then, after the Lord had spoken to them, He was received up into heaven, and sat down at the right hand of God.

Acts 1:11 who also said, "Men of Galilee, why do you stand gazing up into heaven? This same Jesus, who was taken up from you into heaven, will so come in like manner as you saw Him go into heaven."

Acts 17:31 because He has appointed a day on which He will judge the world in righteousness by the Man whom He has ordained. He has given assurance of this to all by raising Him from the dead.

QUESTION 29

ORIGINAL

Q. 29. How are we made partakers of the redemption purchased by Christ?

A. We are made partakers of the redemption purchased by Christ, by the effectual application of it to us by his Holy Spirit.

MODERN

Q. 29. How do we share in the redemption which Christ purchased for us?

A. The Holy Spirit works redemption in us. Our redemption has been purchased by Christ, and it is applied to us by the Holy Spirit.

PROOF TEXTS

John 1:11-12 He came to His own, and His own did not receive Him. But as many as received Him, to them He gave the right to become children of God, to those who believe in His name.

Titus 3:5-6 not by works of righteousness which we have done, but according to His mercy He saved us, through the washing of regeneration and renewing of the Holy Spirit, whom He poured out on us abundantly through Jesus Christ our Savior.

QUESTION 30

ORIGINAL

Q. 30. How doth the Spirit apply to us the redemption purchased by Christ?

A. The Spirit applieth to us the redemption purchased by Christ, by working faith in us, and thereby uniting us to Christ in our effectual calling.

MODERN

Q. 30. How does the Holy Spirit apply the redemption purchased by Christ to us?

A. The Holy Spirit joins us with Christ by building faith in us. We refer to this as our *effectual calling*.

PROOF TEXTS
Ephesians 1:13-14 In Him you also trusted, after you heard the word of truth, the gospel of your salvation; in whom also, having believed, you were sealed with the Holy Spirit of promise, who is the guarantee of our inheritance until the redemption of the purchased possession, to the praise of His glory.
John 6:37 All that the Father gives Me will come to Me, and the one who comes to Me I will by no means cast out.
Ephesians 2:8 For by grace you have been saved through faith, and that not of yourselves; it is the gift of God
I Corinthians 1:9 God is faithful, by whom you were called into the fellowship of His Son, Jesus Christ our Lord.

QUESTION 31

ORIGINAL

Q. 31. What is effectual calling?

A. Effectual calling is the work of God's Spirit, whereby, convincing us of our sin and misery, enlightening our minds in the knowledge of Christ, and renewing our wills, he doth persuade and enable us to embrace Jesus Christ, freely offered to us in the gospel.

MODERN

Q. 31. What is effectual calling?

A. Effectual calling is the work of the Holy Spirit in our hearts and minds. The Spirit convinces us that we are miserable sinners, and He opens our minds so that we may know Christ. The Spirit also persuades us to accept Jesus Christ, who is freely offered to us in the gospel.

PROOF TEXTS

II Timothy 1:9 who has saved us and called us with a holy calling, not according to our works, but according to His own purpose and grace which was given to us in Christ Jesus before time began

Acts 26:18 to open their eyes, in order to turn them from darkness to light, and from the power of Satan to God, that they may receive forgiveness of sins and an inheritance among those who are sanctified by faith in Me.

Ezekiel 36:26-27 I will give you a new heart and put a new spirit within you; I will take the heart of stone out of your flesh and give you a heart of flesh. I will put My Spirit within you and cause you to walk in My statutes, and you will keep My judgments and do them.

John 6:44-45 No one can come to Me unless the Father who sent Me draws him; and I will raise him up at the last day. It is written in the prophets, 'And they shall all be taught by God.' Therefore everyone who has heard and learned from the Father comes to Me.

Philippians 2:13 for it is God who works in you both to will and to do for His good pleasure.

QUESTION 32

ORIGINAL

Q. 32. What benefits do they that are effectually called partake of in this life?

A. They that are effectually called do in this life partake of justification, adoption, and sanctification, and the several benefits which in this life do either accompany or flow from them.

MODERN

Q. 32. What benefits are received in this life by those who are effectually called?

A. Those people who are effectually called receive justification, adoption, and sanctification during their lifetime on earth. There are additional benefits which result from or occur alongside justification, adoption, and sanctification.

PROOF TEXTS

Romans 8:30 Moreover whom He predestined, these He also called; whom He called, these He also justified; and whom He justified, these He also glorified.

Ephesians 1:5 having predestined us to adoption as sons by Jesus Christ to Himself, according to the good pleasure of His will

I Corinthians 1:30 But of Him you are in Christ Jesus, who became for us wisdom from God—and righteousness and sanctification and redemption

QUESTION 33

ORIGINAL

Q. 33. What is justification?

A. Justification is an act of God's free grace, wherein he pardoneth all our sins, and accepteth us as righteous in his sight, only for the righteousness of Christ imputed to us, and received by faith alone.

MODERN

Q. 33. What is justification?

A. Justification occurs when God (from His own free grace) forgives all our sins and accepts us as righteous in His sight. He does this because of the righteousness of Christ accredited to us. We receive justification only by faith.

PROOF TEXTS

Romans 3:24-25 being justified freely by His grace through the redemption that is in Christ Jesus, whom God set forth as a propitiation by His blood, through faith, to demonstrate His righteousness, because in His forbearance God had passed over the sins that were previously committed

Romans 4:6-8 just as David also describes the blessedness of the man to whom God imputes righteousness apart from works: "Blessed are those whose lawless deeds are forgiven, and whose sins are covered; blessed is the man to whom the LORD shall not impute sin."

II Corinthians 5:19 that is, that God was in Christ reconciling the world to Himself, not imputing their trespasses to them, and has committed to us the word of reconciliation.

II Corinthians 5:21 For He made Him who knew no sin to be sin for us, that we might become the righteousness of God in Him.

Romans 5:17-19 (For if by the one man's offense death reigned through the one, much more those who receive abundance of grace and of the gift of righteousness will reign in life through the One, Jesus Christ.) Therefore, as through one man's offense judgment came to all men, resulting in condemnation, even so through one Man's righteous act the free gift came to all men, resulting in justification of life. For as by one man's disobedience many were made sinners, so also by one Man's obedience many will be made righteous.

Galatians 2:16 knowing that a man is not justified by the works of the law but by faith in Jesus Christ, even we have believed in Christ Jesus, that we might be justified by faith in Christ and not by the works of the law; for by the works of the law no flesh shall be justified.

QUESTION 34

ORIGINAL

Q. 34. What is adoption?

A. Adoption is an act of God's free grace, whereby we are received into the number, and have a right to all the privileges of the sons of God.

MODERN

Q. 34. What is adoption?

A. Adoption occurs when God (from His own free grace) accepts us as His children and makes us His heirs.

PROOF TEXTS
I John 3:1 Behold what manner of love the Father has bestowed on us, that we should be called children of God! Therefore the world does not know us, because it did not know Him.
John 1:12 But as many as received Him, to them He gave the right to become children of God, to those who believe in His name
Romans 8:17 and if children, then heirs—heirs of God and joint heirs with Christ, if indeed we suffer with Him, that we may also be glorified together.

QUESTION 35

ORIGINAL

Q. 35. What is sanctification?

A. Sanctification is the work of God's free grace, whereby we are renewed in the whole man after the image of God, and are enabled more and more to die unto sin, and live unto righteousness.

MODERN

Q. 35. What is sanctification?

A. Sanctification occurs when God (from His own free grace) renews us in His image. Over time, God makes us increasingly able to resist sin and to live in righteousness.

> **PROOF TEXTS**
>
> **II Thessalonians 2:13** But we are bound to give thanks to God always for you, brethren beloved by the Lord, because God from the beginning chose you for salvation through sanctification by the Spirit and belief in the truth
>
> **Ephesians 4: 23-24** and be renewed in the spirit of your mind, and that you put on the new man which was created according to God, in true righteousness and holiness.
>
> **Romans 6:4** Therefore we were buried with Him through baptism into death, that just as Christ was raised from the dead by the glory of the Father, even so we also should walk in newness of life.
>
> **Romans 6:6** knowing this, that our old man was crucified with Him, that the body of sin might be done away with, that we should no longer be slaves of sin.

QUESTION 36

ORIGINAL

Q. 36. What are the benefits which in this life do accompany or flow from justification, adoption, and sanctification?

A. The benefits which in this life do accompany or flow from justification, adoption, and sanctification, are, assurance of God's love, peace of conscience, joy in the Holy Ghost, increase of grace, and perseverance therein to the end.

MODERN

Q. 36. What are the other benefits we receive during this life which result from or occur alongside justification, adoption, and sanctification?

A. Other benefits received during our lifetime on earth include: assurance of God's love for us, peace within our conscience, joy in the Holy Spirit, increasing grace, and persistence in faith by God's grace to the end of life.

PROOF TEXTS

Romans 5:1-2 Therefore, having been justified by faith, we have peace with God through our Lord Jesus Christ, through whom also we have access by faith into this grace in which we stand, and rejoice in hope of the glory of God.

Romans 5:5 Now hope does not disappoint, because the love of God has been poured out in our hearts by the Holy Spirit who was given to us.

Romans 14:17 for the kingdom of God is not eating and drinking, but righteousness and peace and joy in the Holy Spirit.

Proverbs 4:18 But the path of the just is like the shining sun, that shines ever brighter unto the perfect day.

I John 5:13 These things I have written to you who believe in the name of the Son of God, that you may know that you have eternal life, and that you may continue to believe in the name of the Son of God.

I Peter 1:5 who are kept by the power of God through faith for salvation ready to be revealed in the last time.

QUESTION 37

ORIGINAL

Q. 37. What benefits do believers receive from Christ at death?

A. The souls of believers are at their death made perfect in holiness, and do immediately pass into glory; and their bodies, being still united to Christ, do rest in their graves till the resurrection.

MODERN

Q. 37. What help do we receive from Christ when we die?

A. When believers die, their souls are made perfectly holy. In this state of perfection, they are immediately received into heaven. Their bodies (still united with Christ) rest in their graves until the day of resurrection.

PROOF TEXTS
II Corinthians 5:1 For we know that if our earthly house, this tent, is destroyed, we have a building from God, a house not made with hands, eternal in the heavens. **II Corinthians 5:8** We are confident, yes, well pleased rather to be absent from the body and to be present with the Lord. **Philippians 1:23** For I am hard-pressed between the two, having a desire to depart and be with Christ, which is far better. **Luke 23:43** And Jesus said to him, "Assuredly, I say to you, today you will be with Me in Paradise."

I Thessalonians 4:14 For if we believe that Jesus died and rose again, even so God will bring with Him those who sleep in Jesus.

Job 19:26-27 And after my skin is destroyed, this I know, that in my flesh I shall see God, whom I shall see for myself, and my eyes shall behold, and not another. How my heart yearns within me!

QUESTION 38

ORIGINAL

Q. 38. What benefits do believers receive from Christ at the resurrection?

A. At the resurrection, believers being raised up in glory, shall be openly acknowledged and acquitted in the day of judgment, and made perfectly blessed in the full enjoying of God to all eternity.

MODERN

Q. 38. What assistance do believers receive from Christ on the day of resurrection?

A. On the day of resurrection, believers will be raised up in glory. At the judgment, they will be openly accepted by God. Because of Christ, believers will be proclaimed innocent of all sin. Afterward, they will be blessed with the full enjoyment of God throughout eternity.

> **PROOF TEXTS**
>
> **I Corinthians 15:43** It is sown in dishonor, it is raised in glory. It is sown in weakness, it is raised in power.
>
> **Matthew 25:23** His lord said to him, 'Well done, good and faithful servant; you have been faithful over a few things, I will make you ruler over many things. Enter into the joy of your lord.'
>
> **Matthew 10:32** Therefore whoever confesses Me before men, him I will also confess before My Father who is in heaven.

I John 3:2 Beloved, now we are children of God; and it has not yet been revealed what we shall be, but we know that when He is revealed, we shall be like Him, for we shall see Him as He is.

I Corinthians 13:12 For now we see in a mirror, dimly, but then face to face. Now I know in part, but then I shall know just as I also am known.

I Thessalonians 4:17-18 Then we who are alive and remain shall be caught up together with them in the clouds to meet the Lord in the air. And thus we shall always be with the Lord. Therefore comfort one another with these words.

QUESTION 39

ORIGINAL

Q. 39. What is the duty which God requireth of man?

A. The duty which God requireth of man, is obedience to his revealed will.

MODERN

Q. 39. What is our responsibility before God?

A. God has revealed certain things which He requires of us, and it is our responsibility to obey Him.

> **PROOF TEXTS**
>
> **Micah 6:8** He has shown you, O man, what is good; and what does the LORD require of you but to do justly, to love mercy, and to walk humbly with your God?
>
> **I Samuel 15:22** So Samuel said: "Has the LORD as great delight in burnt offerings and sacrifices, as in obeying the voice of the LORD? Behold, to obey is better than sacrifice, and to heed than the fat of rams."

QUESTION 40

ORIGINAL

Q. 40. What did God at first reveal to man for the rule of his obedience?

A. The rule which God at first revealed to man for his obedience, was the moral law.

MODERN

Q. 40. What was the first set of rules which God revealed to mankind?

A. The moral law was the first set of rules revealed by God, and we are required to obey it.

PROOF TEXTS
Romans 2:14-15 for when Gentiles, who do not have the law, by nature do the things in the law, these, although not having the law, are a law to themselves, who show the work of the law written in their hearts, their conscience also bearing witness, and between themselves their thoughts accusing or else excusing them
Romans 10:5 For Moses writes about the righteousness which is of the law, "The man who does those things shall live by them."

QUESTION 41

ORIGINAL

Q. 41. Where is the moral law summarily comprehended?

A. The moral law is summarily comprehended in the ten commandments.

MODERN

Q. 41. Where can we find a summary of the moral law?

A. We can find a summary of the moral law in the Ten Commandments.

PROOF TEXTS
Deuteronomy 10:4 And He wrote on the tablets according to the first writing, the Ten Commandments, which the LORD had spoken to you in the mountain from the midst of the fire in the day of the assembly; and the LORD gave them to me.

QUESTION 42

ORIGINAL

Q. 42. What is the sum of the ten commandments?

A. The sum of the ten commandments is, *To love the Lord our God with all our heart, with all our soul, with all our strength, and with all our mind; and our neighbor as ourselves.*

MODERN

Q. 42. How can we summarize the Ten Commandments?

A. A summary of the Ten Commandments is as follows: *"You shall love the LORD your God will all your heart, with all your soul, with all your mind, and with all your strength,"* and *"you shall love you neighbor as yourself."*

PROOF TEXTS

Matthew 22:37-40 Jesus said to him, "'You shall love the LORD your God with all your heart, with all your soul, and with all your mind.' This is the first and great commandment. And the second is like it: 'You shall love your neighbor as yourself.' On these two commandments hang all the Law and the Prophets."

QUESTION 43

ORIGINAL

Q. 43. What is the preface to the ten commandments?

A. The preface to the ten commandments is in these words, *I am the Lord thy God, which have brought thee out of the land of Egypt, out of the house of bondage.*

MODERN

Q. 43. What is the introduction to the Ten Commandments?

A. The introduction to the Ten Commandments is as follows: *"I am the LORD your God, who brought you out of the land of Egypt, out of the house of bondage."*

> **PROOF TEXTS**
>
> **Exodus 20:2** I am the LORD your God, who brought you out of the land of Egypt, out of the house of bondage.

QUESTION 44

ORIGINAL

Q. 44. What doth the preface to the ten commandments teach us?

A. The preface to the ten commandments teacheth us, That because God is the Lord, and our God, and Redeemer, therefore we are bound to keep all his commandments.

MODERN

Q. 44. What does the introduction to the Ten Commandments teach us?

A. The introduction reminds us that God is our Lord, our God, and our Redeemer. Therefore, we must obey His commandments.

> **PROOF TEXTS**
>
> **Luke 1:74-75** To grant us that we, being delivered from the hand of our enemies, might serve Him without fear, in holiness and righteousness before Him all the days of our life.
>
> **I Peter 1:15-19** but as He who called you is holy, you also be holy in all your conduct, because it is written, "Be holy, for I am holy." And if you call on the Father, who without partiality judges according to each one's work, conduct yourselves throughout the time of your stay here in fear; knowing that you were not redeemed with corruptible things, like silver or gold, from your aimless conduct received by tradition from your fathers, but with the precious blood of Christ, as of a lamb without blemish and without spot.

QUESTION 45

ORIGINAL

Q. 45. Which is the first commandment?

A. The first commandment is, *Thou shalt have no other gods before me.*

MODERN

Q. 45. What is the first commandment?

A. The first commandment is: *"You shall have no other gods before Me."*

PROOF TEXTS
Exodus 20:3 You shall have no other gods before Me.

QUESTION 46

ORIGINAL

Q. 46. What is required in the first commandment?

A. The first commandment requireth us to know and acknowledge God to be the only true God, and our God; and to worship and glorify him accordingly.

MODERN

Q. 46. What does the first commandment require of us?

A. The first commandment requires that we recognize that God is the only true God and that He is our God. We must worship and glorify Him in a manner which acknowledges Him as our Lord.

> **PROOF TEXTS**
>
> **Deuteronomy 26:17** Today you have proclaimed the LORD to be your God, and that you will walk in His ways and keep His statutes, His commandments, and His judgments, and that you will obey His voice.
>
> **Matthew 4:10** Then Jesus said to him, "Away with you, Satan! For it is written, 'You shall worship the LORD your God, and Him only you shall serve.'"
>
> **Psalm 29:2** Give unto the LORD the glory due to His name; worship the LORD in the beauty of holiness.

QUESTION 47

ORIGINAL

Q. 47. What is forbidden in the first commandment?

A. The first commandment forbiddeth the denying, or not worshipping and glorifying the true God as God, and our God; and the giving of that worship and glory to any other, which is due to him alone.

MODERN

Q. 47. What is forbidden in the first commandment?

A. The first commandment forbids denying the existence of God or refusing to worship and glorify Him. It also forbids worshiping or glorifying anything else in a manner which should be reserved for God alone.

PROOF TEXTS

Psalm 14:1 The fool has said in his heart, "There is no God." They are corrupt, they have done abominable works, there is none who does good.

Romans 1:21 because, although they knew God, they did not glorify Him as God, nor were thankful, but became futile in their thoughts, and their foolish hearts were darkened.

Romans 1:25-26 who exchanged the truth of God for the lie, and worshiped and served the creature rather than the Creator, who is blessed forever. Amen. For this reason God gave them up to vile passions. For even their women exchanged the natural use for what is against nature.

QUESTION 48

ORIGINAL

Q. 48. What are we specially taught by these words, *before me* in the first commandment?

A. These words *before me* in the first commandment teach us, That God, who seeth all things, taketh notice of, and is much displeased with, the sin of having any other God.

MODERN

Q. 48. The first commandment uses the phrase *"before Me."* What does this mean?

A. The phrase *"before Me"* reminds us that God sees everything. We must realize that He notices when we worship other gods, and He is very displeased.

> **PROOF TEXTS**
>
> **Ezekiel 8:9-12** And He said to me, "Go in, and see the wicked abominations which they are doing there." So I went in and saw, and there—every sort of creeping thing, abominable beasts, and all the idols of the house of Israel, portrayed all around on the walls. And there stood before them seventy men of the elders of the house of Israel, and in their midst stood Jaazaniah the son of Shaphan. Each man had a censer in his hand, and a thick cloud of incense went up. Then He said to me, "Son of man, have you seen what the elders of the house of Israel do in the dark, every man in the room of his idols? For they say, 'The LORD does not see us, the LORD has forsaken the land.'"

QUESTION 49

ORIGINAL

Q. 49. Which is the second commandment?

A. The second commandment is, *Thou shalt not make unto thee any graven image, or any likeness of any thing that is in heaven above, or that is in the earth beneath, or that is in the water under the earth. Thou shalt not bow down thyself to them, nor serve them: for I the Lord thy God am a jealous God, visiting the iniquity of the fathers upon the children unto the third and fourth generation of them that hate me; and showing mercy unto thousands of them that love me, and keep my commandments.*

MODERN

Q. 49. What is the second commandment?

A. The second commandment is: *"You shall not make for yourself a carved image—any likeness of anything that is in heaven above, or that is in the earth beneath, or that is in the water under the earth; you shall not bow down to them nor serve them. For I, the LORD your God, am a jealous God, visiting the iniquity of the fathers upon the children to the third and fourth generations of those who hate Me, but showing mercy to thousands, to those who love Me and keep My commandments."*

PROOF TEXTS

Exodus 20:4-6 You shall not make for yourself a carved image—any likeness of anything that is in heaven above, or that is in the earth beneath, or that is in the water under the earth; you shall not bow down to them nor serve them. For I, the LORD your God, am a jealous God, visiting the iniquity of the fathers upon the children to the third and fourth generations of those who hate Me, but showing mercy to thousands, to those who love Me and keep My commandments.

QUESTION 50

ORIGINAL

Q. 50. What is required in the second commandment?

A. The second commandment requireth the receiving, observing, and keeping pure and entire, all such religious worship and ordinances as God hath appointed in his Word.

MODERN

Q. 50. What does the second commandment require of us?

A. The second commandment requires that we worship God in the manner in which He has instructed us to worship Him. We should do this completely and without compromise.

PROOF TEXTS
Deuteronomy 32:46 and he said to them: "Set your hearts on all the words which I testify among you today, which you shall command your children to be careful to observe—all the words of this law."
Acts 2:42 And they continued steadfastly in the apostles' doctrine and fellowship, in the breaking of bread, and in prayers.

QUESTION 51

ORIGINAL

Q. 51. What is forbidden in the second commandment?

A. The second commandment forbiddeth the worshipping of God by images, or any other way not appointed in his Word.

MODERN

Q. 51. What is forbidden in the second commandment?

A. The second commandment forbids worshiping God through an image. It also forbids any other type of worship which is not expressly required by Scripture.

PROOF TEXTS
Deuteronomy 4:15-19 Take careful heed to yourselves, for you saw no form when the LORD spoke to you at Horeb out of the midst of the fire, lest you act corruptly and make for yourselves a carved image in the form of any figure: the likeness of male or female, the likeness of any animal that is on the earth or the likeness of any winged bird that flies in the air, the likeness of anything that creeps on the ground or the likeness of any fish that is in the water beneath the earth. And take heed, lest you lift your eyes to heaven, and when you see the sun, the moon, and the stars, all the host of heaven, you feel driven to worship them and serve them, which the LORD your God has given to all the peoples under the whole heaven as a heritage.

QUESTION 52

ORIGINAL

Q. 52. What are the reasons annexed to the second commandment?

A. The reasons annexed to the second commandment are, God's sovereignty over us, his propriety in us, and the zeal he hath to his own worship.

MODERN

Q. 52. There are reasons assigned to the second commandment. What do these reasons teach us?

A. The reasons attached to the second commandment teach us that God is our Lord and that our worship belongs to Him. He is passionate about our worship of Him.

PROOF TEXTS
Psalm 95:2-3 Let us come before His presence with thanksgiving; let us shout joyfully to Him with psalms. For the LORD is the great God, and the great King above all gods.
Psalm 95:6 Oh come, let us worship and bow down; let us kneel before the LORD our Maker.
Exodus 34:13-14 But you shall destroy their altars, break their sacred pillars, and cut down their wooden images (for you shall worship no other god, for the LORD, whose name is Jealous, is a jealous God).

QUESTION 53

ORIGINAL

Q. 53. Which is the third commandment?

A. The third commandment is, *Thou shalt not take the name of the Lord thy God in vain; for the Lord will not hold him guiltless that taketh his name in vain.*

MODERN

Q. 53. What is the third commandment?

A. The third commandment is as follows: *"You shall not take the name of the LORD your God in vain, for the LORD will not hold him guiltless who takes His name in vain."*

> **PROOF TEXTS**
>
> **Exodus 20:7** You shall not take the name of the LORD your God in vain, for the LORD will not hold him guiltless who takes His name in vain.

QUESTION 54

ORIGINAL

Q. 54. What is required in the third commandment?

A. The third commandment requireth the holy and reverent use of God's names, titles, attributes, ordinances, Word, and works.

MODERN

Q. 54. What does the third commandment require of us?

A. The third commandment requires that we respect God's name, titles, characteristics, laws, Word, and works.

> **PROOF TEXTS**
>
> **Deuteronomy 28:58** If you do not carefully observe all the words of this law that are written in this book, that you may fear this glorious and awesome name, THE LORD YOUR GOD.
>
> **Revelation 15:3-4** They sing the song of Moses, the servant of God, and the song of the Lamb, saying: "Great and marvelous are Your works, Lord God Almighty! Just and true are Your ways, O King of the saints! Who shall not fear You, O Lord, and glorify Your name? For You alone are holy. For all nations shall come and worship before You, for Your judgments have been manifested."
>
> **Malachi 1:11** "For from the rising of the sun, even to its going down, My name shall be great among the Gentiles; in every place incense shall be offered to My name, and a pure

offering; for My name shall be great among the nations," says the Lord of hosts.

Psalm 138:1-2 I will praise You with my whole heart; before the gods I will sing praises to You. I will worship toward Your holy temple, and praise Your name for Your lovingkindness and Your truth; for You have magnified Your word above all Your name.

Job 36:24 Remember to magnify His work, of which men have sung.

Matthew 6:9 In this manner, therefore, pray: Our Father in heaven, hallowed be Your name.

QUESTION 55

ORIGINAL

Q. 55. What is forbidden in the third commandment?

A. The third commandment forbiddeth all profaning and abusing of anything whereby God maketh himself known.

MODERN

Q. 55. What does the third commandment forbid?

A. The third commandment forbids misusing or showing any disrespect for God, His name, or the ways in which He makes Himself known to us.

> **PROOF TEXTS**
>
> **Malachi 1:12** But you profane it, in that you say, 'The table of the LORD is defiled; and its fruit, its food, is contemptible.'
>
> **Malachi 2:2** "If you will not hear, and if you will not take it to heart, to give glory to My name," says the LORD of hosts, "I will send a curse upon you, and I will curse your blessings. Yes, I have cursed them already, because you do not take it to heart."

QUESTION 56

ORIGINAL

Q. 56. What is the reason annexed to the third commandment?

A. The reason annexed to the third commandment is, That however the breakers of this commandment may escape punishment from men, yet the Lord our God will not suffer them to escape his righteous judgment.

MODERN

Q. 56. There is a reason attached to the third commandment. What is that reason?

A. The reason attached to the third commandment is that God will punish those who break it, even if they receive no punishment from other people.

PROOF TEXTS

I Samuel 2:29 Why do you kick at My sacrifice and My offering which I have commanded in My dwelling place, and honor your sons more than Me, to make yourselves fat with the best of all the offerings of Israel My people?

Deuteronomy 28:58-59 If you do not carefully observe all the words of this law that are written in this book, that you may fear this glorious and awesome name, THE LORD YOUR GOD, then the LORD will bring upon you and your descendants extraordinary plagues—great and prolonged plagues—and serious and prolonged sicknesses.

QUESTION 57

ORIGINAL

Q. 57. Which is the fourth commandment?

A. The fourth commandment is, *Remember the Sabbath-day, to keep it holy. Six days shalt thou labour, and do all thy work; but the seventh day is the Sabbath of the Lord thy God: in it thou shalt not do any work, thou, nor thy son, nor thy daughter, thy man-servant, nor thy maid-servant, nor thy cattle, nor thy stranger that is within thy gates. For in six days the Lord made heaven and earth, the sea, and all that in them is, and rested the seventh day: wherefore the Lord blessed the Sabbath day, and hallowed it.*

MODERN

Q. 57. What is the fourth commandment?

A. The fourth commandment is as follows: "Remember the Sabbath day, to keep it holy. Six days you shall labor and do all your work, but the seventh day is the Sabbath of the LORD your God. In it you shall do no work: you, nor your son, nor your daughter, nor your male servant, nor your female servant, nor your cattle, nor your stranger who is within your gates. For in six days the LORD made the heavens and the earth, the sea, and all that is in them, and rested the seventh day. Therefore the LORD blessed the Sabbath day and hallowed it."

> **PROOF TEXTS**
>
> **Exodus 20:8-11** Remember the Sabbath day, to keep it holy. Six days you shall labor and do all your work, but the seventh day is the Sabbath of the LORD your God. In it you shall do no work: you, nor your son, nor your daughter, nor your male servant, nor your female servant, nor your cattle, nor your stranger who is within your gates. For in six days the LORD made the heavens and the earth, the sea, and all that is in them, and rested the seventh day. Therefore the LORD blessed the Sabbath day and hallowed it.

QUESTION 58

ORIGINAL

Q. 58. What is required in the fourth commandment?

A. The fourth commandment requireth the keeping holy to God such set times as he hath appointed in his Word; expressly one whole day in seven, to be a holy Sabbath to himself.

MODERN

Q. 58. What does the fourth commandment require of us?

A. The fourth commandment requires that we set aside the Sabbath day as God has taught us, and that we keep it as the Lord's day.

> **PROOF TEXTS**
>
> **Deuteronomy 15:12-14** Observe the Sabbath day, to keep it holy, as the LORD your God commanded you. Six days you shall labor and do all your work, but the seventh day is the Sabbath of the LORD your God. In it you shall do no work: you, nor your son, nor your daughter, nor your male servant, nor your female servant, nor your ox, nor your donkey, nor any of your cattle, nor your stranger who is within your gates, that your male servant and your female servant may rest as well as you.

QUESTION 59

ORIGINAL

Q. 59. Which day of the seven hath God appointed to be the weekly Sabbath?

A. From the beginning of the world to the resurrection of Christ, God appointed the seventh day of the week to be the weekly Sabbath; and the first day of the week ever since, to continue to the end of the world, which is the Christian Sabbath.

MODERN

Q. 59. Which day of the week should we set aside as the Sabbath day?

A. From the beginning of the world until the resurrection of Christ, God appointed the seventh day of the week (Saturday) as the Sabbath. However, since the resurrection of Christ, the newly appointed day is the first day of the week (Sunday). This is the Christian Sabbath, and it will continue to be so until the end of the world.

> **PROOF TEXTS**
>
> **Genesis 2:2-3** And on the seventh day God ended His work which He had done, and He rested on the seventh day from all His work which He had done. Then God blessed the seventh day and sanctified it, because in it He rested from all His work which God had created and made.
>
> **Acts 20:7** Now on the first day of the week, when the disciples came together to break bread, Paul, ready to depart the next day, spoke to them and continued his message until midnight.

QUESTION 60

ORIGINAL

Q. 60. How is the Sabbath to be sanctified?

A. The Sabbath is to be sanctified by a holy resting all that day, even from such worldly employments and recreations as are lawful on other days; and spending the whole time in the public and private exercises of God's worship, except so much as is to be taken up in the works of necessity and mercy.

MODERN

Q. 60. How should we keep the Sabbath holy?

A. We should keep the Sabbath holy by resting on that day. We must not work or even engage in the same type of recreation as we do on other days. We are commanded to spend the Sabbath in the worship of God, both at church and at home. The only exception to this rule is that we are permitted to do things which are necessary or are acts of kindness toward others.

> **PROOF TEXTS**
>
> **Exodus 16:25-28** Then Moses said, "Eat that today, for today is a Sabbath to the LORD; today you will not find it in the field. Six days you shall gather it, but on the seventh day, the Sabbath, there will be none." Now it happened that some of the people went out on the seventh day to gather, but they found none. And the LORD said to Moses, "How long do you refuse to keep My commandments and My laws?"

Nehemiah 13:15-19 In those days I saw people in Judah treading wine presses on the Sabbath, and bringing in sheaves, and loading donkeys with wine, grapes, figs, and all kinds of burdens, which they brought into Jerusalem on the Sabbath day. And I warned them about the day on which they were selling provisions. Men of Tyre dwelt there also, who brought in fish and all kinds of goods, and sold them on the Sabbath to the children of Judah, and in Jerusalem. Then I contended with the nobles of Judah, and said to them, "What evil thing is this that you do, by which you profane the Sabbath day? Did not your fathers do thus, and did not our God bring all this disaster on us and on this city? Yet you bring added wrath on Israel by profaning the Sabbath." So it was, at the gates of Jerusalem, as it began to be dark before the Sabbath, that I commanded the gates to be shut, and charged that they must not be opened till after the Sabbath. Then I posted some of my servants at the gates, so that no burdens would be brought in on the Sabbath day.

Luke 4:16 So He came to Nazareth, where He had been brought up. And as His custom was, He went into the synagogue on the Sabbath day, and stood up to read.

Matthew 12:1-14 At that time Jesus went through the grainfields on the Sabbath. And His disciples were hungry, and began to pluck heads of grain and to eat. And when the Pharisees saw it, they said to Him, "Look, Your disciples are doing what is not lawful to do on the Sabbath!" But He said to them, "Have you not read what David did when he was hungry, he and those who were with him: how he entered the house of God and ate the showbread which was not lawful for him to eat, nor for those who were with him, but only for the priests? Or have you not read in the law that on the Sabbath the priests in the temple profane the Sabbath, and are blameless? Yet I say to you that in this place there is One greater than the temple. But if you had known what this means, 'I desire mercy and not sacrifice,' you would not have condemned the guiltless. For the Son of Man is Lord even of the Sabbath."

Now when He had departed from there, He went into their synagogue. And behold, there was a man who had a withered hand. And they asked Him, saying, "Is it lawful to heal on the Sabbath?"—that they might accuse Him. Then He said to them, "What man is there among you who has one sheep, and if it falls into a pit on the Sabbath, will not lay hold of it and lift it out? Of how much more value then is a man than a sheep? Therefore it is lawful to do good on the Sabbath." Then He said to the man, "Stretch out your hand." And he stretched it out, and it was restored as whole as the other. Then the Pharisees went out and plotted against Him, how they might destroy Him.

QUESTION 61

ORIGINAL

Q. 61. What is forbidden in the fourth commandment?

A. The fourth commandment forbiddeth the omission or careless performance of the duties required, and the profaning the day by idleness, or doing that which is in itself sinful, or by unnecessary thoughts, words, or works, about our worldly employments or recreations.

MODERN

Q. 61. What does the fourth commandment forbid?

A. The fourth commandment forbids us to be neglectful or careless in our Sabbath duties. We must not be lazy, and we certainly may not engage in sinful activities. We also should not speak about (or mentally plan) our weekday work or recreation.

PROOF TEXTS

Ezekiel 22:26 Her priests have violated My law and profaned My holy things; they have not distinguished between the holy and unholy, nor have they made known the difference between the unclean and the clean; and they have hidden their eyes from My Sabbaths, so that I am profaned among them.

Ezekiel 23:38 Moreover they have done this to Me: They have defiled My sanctuary on the same day and profaned My Sabbaths.

Amos 8:5 Saying: "When will the New Moon be past, that we may sell grain? And the Sabbath, that we may trade wheat? Making the ephah small and the shekel large, falsifying the scales by deceit

Jeremiah 17:24-26 "And it shall be, if you heed Me carefully," says the LORD, "to bring no burden through the gates of this city on the Sabbath day, but hallow the Sabbath day, to do no work in it, then shall enter the gates of this city kings and princes sitting on the throne of David, riding in chariots and on horses, they and their princes, accompanied by the men of Judah and the inhabitants of Jerusalem; and this city shall remain forever. And they shall come from the cities of Judah and from the places around Jerusalem, from the land of Benjamin and from the lowland, from the mountains and from the South, bringing burnt offerings and sacrifices, grain offerings and incense, bringing sacrifices of praise to the house of the LORD."

QUESTION 62

ORIGINAL

Q. 62. What are the reasons annexed to the fourth commandment?

A. The reasons annexed to the fourth commandment are, God's allowing us six days of the week for our own employments, his challenging a special propriety in the seventh, his own example, and his blessing the sabbath-day.

MODERN

Q. 62. What are the reasons assigned to the fourth commandments?

A. The reasons assigned to the fourth commandment are as follows: God has given us six days of the week for work, but He claims one day for Himself. By His own example, He has shown that the Sabbath is holy, and He has blessed it.

PROOF TEXTS

Exodus 20:11 For in six days the LORD made the heavens and the earth, the sea, and all that is in them, and rested the seventh day. Therefore the LORD blessed the Sabbath day and hallowed it.

QUESTION 63

ORIGINAL

Q. 63. Which is the fifth commandment?

A. The fifth commandment is, *Honour thy father and thy mother; that thy days may be long upon the land which the Lord thy God giveth thee.*

MODERN

Q. 63. What is the fifth commandment?

A. The fifth commandment is: *"Honor your father and your mother, that your days may be long upon the land which the LORD your God is giving you."*

> **PROOF TEXTS**
>
> **Exodus 20:12** Honor your father and your mother, that your days may be long upon the land which the LORD your God is giving you.

QUESTION 64

ORIGINAL

Q. 64. What is required in the fifth commandment?

A. The fifth commandment requireth the preserving the honour, and performing the duties, belonging to every one in their several places and relations, as superiors, inferiors, or equals.

MODERN

Q. 64. What does the fifth commandment require us to do?

A. The fifth commandment requires us to respect others. Whether they are above, below, or equal in their relationship to us, we should be mindful of our responsibility toward them.

> **PROOF TEXTS**
>
> **Ephesians 5:21** submitting to one another in the fear of God.
>
> **I Peter 2:17** Honor all people. Love the brotherhood. Fear God. Honor the king.
>
> **Romans 12:10** Be kindly affectionate to one another with brotherly love, in honor giving preference to one another

QUESTION 65

ORIGINAL

Q. 65. What is the forbidden in the fifth commandment?

A. The fifth commandment forbiddeth the neglecting of, or doing anything against, the honour and duty which belongeth to every one in their several places and relations.

MODERN

Q. 65. What does the fifth commandment forbid?

A. The fifth commandment forbids us to show disrespect toward others. It also forbids us to neglect our responsibility toward those around us, whatever their station in life.

PROOF TEXTS

Matthew 15:4-6 For God commanded, saying, 'Honor your father and your mother'; and, 'He who curses father or mother, let him be put to death.' But you say, 'Whoever says to his father or mother, "Whatever profit you might have received from me is a gift to God"—then he need not honor his father or mother.' Thus you have made the commandment of God of no effect by your tradition.

Ezekiel 34:2-4 Son of man, prophesy against the shepherds of Israel, prophesy and say to them, 'Thus says the Lord GOD to the shepherds: "Woe to the shepherds of Israel who feed themselves! Should not the shepherds feed the flocks? You eat the fat and clothe yourselves with the wool; you slaughter the fatlings, but you do not feed the flock. The weak you have not strengthened, nor have you healed those who were sick, nor bound up the broken, nor brought back what was driven away, nor sought what was lost; but with force and cruelty you have ruled them.

Romans 13:8 Owe no one anything except to love one another, for he who loves another has fulfilled the law.

QUESTION 66

ORIGINAL

Q. 66. What is the reason annexed to the fifth commandment?

A. The reason annexed to the fifth commandment, is a promise of long life and prosperity (as far as it shall serve for God's glory and their own good) to all such as keep this commandment.

MODERN

Q. 66. What reason is given for the fifth commandment?

A. The promise of long life and success (to the extent that it serves the glory of God and our own good) is given to all who keep the fifth commandment.

PROOF TEXTS
Deuteronomy 5:16 Honor your father and your mother, as the LORD your God has commanded you, that your days may be long, and that it may be well with you in the land which the LORD your God is giving you.
Ephesians 6:2-3 "Honor your father and mother," which is the first commandment with promise: "that it may be well with you and you may live long on the earth."

QUESTION 67

ORIGINAL

Q. 67. Which is the sixth commandment?

A. The sixth commandment is, Thou shalt not kill.

MODERN

Q. 67. What is the sixth commandment?

A. The sixth commandment is: *"You shall not murder."*

PROOF TEXTS
Exodus 20:13 You shall not murder.

QUESTION 68

ORIGINAL

Q. 68. What is required in the sixth commandment?

A. The sixth commandment requireth all lawful endeavours to preserve our own life, and the life of others.

MODERN

Q. 68. What does the sixth commandment require of us?

A. The sixth commandment requires that we do everything we can (within the law of God) to preserve our own life and the life of others.

PROOF TEXTS
Ephesians 5:28-29 So husbands ought to love their own wives as their own bodies; he who loves his wife loves himself. For no one ever hated his own flesh, but nourishes and cherishes it, just as the Lord does the church.
I Kings 18:4 For so it was, while Jezebel massacred the prophets of the LORD, that Obadiah had taken one hundred prophets and hidden them, fifty to a cave, and had fed them with bread and water.

QUESTION 69

ORIGINAL

Q. 69. What is forbidden in the sixth commandment?

A. The sixth commandment forbiddeth the taking away of our own life, or the life of our neighbour unjustly, or whatsoever tendeth thereunto.

MODERN

Q. 69. What does the sixth commandment forbid?

A. The sixth commandment forbids suicide and murder, as well as anything leading to suicide or murder.

PROOF TEXTS
Acts 16:28 But Paul called with a loud voice, saying, "Do yourself no harm, for we are all here."
Genesis 9:6 Whoever sheds man's blood, by man his blood shall be shed; for in the image of God He made man.

QUESTION 70

ORIGINAL

Q. 70. Which is the seventh commandment?

A. The seventh commandment is, Thou shalt not commit adultery.

MODERN

Q. 70. What is the seventh commandment?

A. The seventh commandment is: *"You shall not commit adultery."*

PROOF TEXTS
Exodus 20:14 You shall not commit adultery.

QUESTION 71

ORIGINAL

Q. 71. What is required in the seventh commandment?

A. The seventh commandment requireth the preservation of our own and our neighbor's chastity, in heart, speech, and behaviour.

MODERN

Q. 71. What does the seventh commandment require of us?

A. The seventh commandment requires that we maintain sexual purity—both our own and that of others—in our thoughts, words, and behavior.

PROOF TEXTS
I Corinthians 7:2-3 Nevertheless, because of sexual immorality, let each man have his own wife, and let each woman have her own husband. Let the husband render to his wife the affection due her, and likewise also the wife to her husband.
I Thessalonians 4:3-5 For this is the will of God, your sanctification: that you should abstain from sexual immorality; that each of you should know how to possess his own vessel in sanctification and honor, not in passion of lust, like the Gentiles who do not know God

QUESTION 72

ORIGINAL

Q. 72. What is forbidden in the seventh commandment?

A. The seventh commandment forbiddeth all unchaste thoughts, words, and actions.

MODERN

Q. 72. What does the seventh commandment forbid?

A. The seventh commandment forbids all sexual impurity in our thoughts, words, and actions.

> **PROOF TEXTS**
>
> **Matthew 5:28** But I say to you that whoever looks at a woman to lust for her has already committed adultery with her in his heart.
>
> **Ephesians 5:3-4** But fornication and all uncleanness or covetousness, let it not even be named among you, as is fitting for saints; neither filthiness, nor foolish talking, nor coarse jesting, which are not fitting, but rather giving of thanks.

QUESTION 73

ORIGINAL

Q. 73. Which is the eighth commandment?

A. The eighth commandment is, *Thou shalt not steal.*

MODERN

Q. 73. What is the eighth commandment?

A. The eighth commandment is: *"You shall not steal."*

PROOF TEXTS
Exodus 20:15 You shall not steal.

QUESTION 74

ORIGINAL

Q. 74. What is required in the eighth commandment?

A. The eighth commandment requireth the lawful procuring and furthering the wealth and outward estate of ourselves and others.

MODERN

Q. 74. What does the eighth commandment require of us?

A. The eighth commandment requires that we lawfully work to increase the wealth and possessions of ourselves and others.

PROOF TEXTS
Leviticus 25:35 If one of your brethren becomes poor, and falls into poverty among you, then you shall help him, like a stranger or a sojourner, that he may live with you.
Ephesians 4:28 Let him who stole steal no longer, but rather let him labor, working with his hands what is good, that he may have something to give him who has need.
Philippians 2:4 Let each of you look out not only for his own interests, but also for the interests of others.

QUESTION 75

ORIGINAL

Q. 75. What is forbidden in the eighth commandment?

A. The eighth commandment forbiddeth whatsoever doth or may unjustly hinder our own or our neighbour's wealth or outward estate.

MODERN

Q. 75. What does the eighth commandment forbid?

A. The eighth commandment forbids doing anything unfairly which leads to loss of money or possessions either for ourselves or anyone else.

> **PROOF TEXTS**
>
> **Proverbs 28:19** He who tills his land will have plenty of bread, but he who follows frivolity will have poverty enough!
>
> **II Thessalonians 3:10** For even when we were with you, we commanded you this: If anyone will not work, neither shall he eat.
>
> **I Timothy 5:8** But if anyone does not provide for his own, and especially for those of his household, he has denied the faith and is worse than an unbeliever.

QUESTION 76

ORIGINAL

Q. 76. What is the ninth commandment?

A. The ninth commandment is, *Thou shalt not bear false witness against thy neighbour.*

MODERN

Q. 76. What is the ninth commandment?

A. The ninth commandment is: *"You shall not bear false witness against your neighbor."*

PROOF TEXTS
Exodus 20:16 You shall not bear false witness against your neighbor.

QUESTION 77

ORIGINAL

Q. 77. What is required in the ninth commandment?

A. The ninth commandment requireth the maintaining and promoting of truth between man and man, and of our own and our neighbour's good name, especially in witness-bearing.

MODERN

Q. 77. What does the ninth commandment require of us?

A. The ninth commandment requires that we be truthful and that we promote truthfulness in regard to reputations (both our own and others'). This is especially important when we testify as witnesses.

PROOF TEXTS

Zechariah 8:16 These are the things you shall do: speak each man the truth to his neighbor; give judgment in your gates for truth, justice, and peace.

III John 1:12 Demetrius has a good testimony from all, and from the truth itself. And we also bear witness, and you know that our testimony is true.

Proverbs 14:25 A true witness delivers souls, but a deceitful witness speaks lies

QUESTION 78

ORIGINAL

Q. 78. What is forbidden in the ninth commandment?

A. The ninth commandment forbiddeth whatsoever is prejudicial to truth, or injurious to our own or our neighbour's good name.

MODERN

Q. 78. What does the ninth commandment forbid?

A. The ninth commandment forbids damaging a reputation (our own or that of someone else) by doing or saying anything untruthful.

> **PROOF TEXTS**
>
> **Leviticus 19:16** You shall not go about as a talebearer among your people; nor shall you take a stand against the life of your neighbor: I am the LORD.
>
> **Psalm 15:3** He who does not backbite with his tongue, nor does evil to his neighbor, nor does he take up a reproach against his friend
>
> **Luke 3:14** Likewise the soldiers asked him, saying, "And what shall we do?" So he said to them, "Do not intimidate anyone or accuse falsely, and be content with your wages."

QUESTION 79

ORIGINAL

Q. 79. Which is the tenth commandment?

A. The tenth commandment is, *Thou shalt not covet thy neighbour's house, thou shalt not covet thy neighbour's wife, nor his manservant, nor his maidservant, nor his ox, nor his ass, nor any thing that is thy neighbour's.*

MODERN

Q. 79. What is the tenth commandment?

A. The tenth commandment is: "You shall not covet your neighbor's house; you shall not covet your neighbor's wife, nor his male servant, nor his female servant, nor his ox, nor his donkey, nor anything that is your neighbor's."

> **PROOF TEXTS**
>
> **Exodus 20:17** You shall not covet your neighbor's house; you shall not covet your neighbor's wife, nor his male servant, nor his female servant, nor his ox, nor his donkey, nor anything that is your neighbor's.

QUESTION 80

ORIGINAL

Q. 80. What is required in the tenth commandment?

A. The tenth commandment requireth full contentment with our own condition, with a right and charitable frame of spirit toward our neighbour, and all that is his.

MODERN

Q. 80. What does the tenth commandment require of us?

A. The tenth commandment requires that we be content with our circumstances. We should behave kindly toward others and respect their property.

PROOF TEXTS
Hebrews 13:5 Let your conduct be without covetousness; be content with such things as you have. For He Himself has said, "I will never leave you nor forsake you."
I Timothy 6:6 Now godliness with contentment is great gain.
I Timothy 1:5 Now the purpose of the commandment is love from a pure heart, from a good conscience, and from sincere faith

QUESTION 81

ORIGINAL

Q. 81. What is forbidden in the tenth commandment?

A. The tenth commandment forbiddeth all discontentment with our own estate, envying or grieving at the good of our neighbour, and all inordinate motions and affections to any thing that is his.

MODERN

Q. 81. What is forbidden in the tenth commandment?

A. The tenth commandment forbids discontented attitudes. We must not be envious of other or be offended when others are successful. We should not crave things which belong to other people.

PROOF TEXTS
I Corinthians 10:10 nor complain, as some of them also complained, and were destroyed by the destroyer.
Galatians 5:26 Let us not become conceited, provoking one another, envying one another.
James 3:16 For where envy and self-seeking exist, confusion and every evil thing are there.

QUESTION 82

ORIGINAL

Q. 82. Is any man able perfectly to keep the commandments of God?

A. No mere man since the fall is able in this life perfectly to keep the commandments of God, but doth daily break them in thought, word, and deed.

MODERN

Q. 82. Is anyone able to keep the laws of God perfectly?

A. No mere human has been able to perfectly keep the law of God in this life since the Fall. We all break God's commandments every day in our thoughts, words, and actions.

PROOF TEXTS

Ecclesiastes 7:20 For there is not a just man on earth who does good and does not sin.

I John 1:8 If we say that we have no sin, we deceive ourselves, and the truth is not in us.

Galatians 5:17 For the flesh lusts against the Spirit, and the Spirit against the flesh; and these are contrary to one another, so that you do not do the things that you wish.

Genesis 8:21 And the LORD smelled a soothing aroma. Then the LORD said in His heart, "I will never again curse the ground for man's sake, although the imagination of man's heart is evil from his youth; nor will I again destroy every living thing as I have done."

Romans 3:9-12 What then? Are we better than they? Not at all. For we have previously charged both Jews and Greeks that they are all under sin. As it is written: "There is none righteous, no, not one; there is none who understands; there is none who seeks after God. They have all turned aside; they have together become unprofitable; there is none who does good, no, not one."

QUESTION 83

ORIGINAL

Q. 83. Are all transgression of the law equally heinous?

A. Some sins in themselves, and by reason of several aggravations, are more heinous in the sight of God than others.

MODERN

Q. 83. Are all sins equally bad?

A. God views some sins as worse than others—either because of the particularly evil nature of those sins or because of other factors which make them worse in particular situations.

> **PROOF TEXTS**
>
> **Ezekiel 8:6** Furthermore He said to me, "Son of man, do you see what they are doing, the great abominations that the house of Israel commits here, to make Me go far away from My sanctuary? Now turn again, you will see greater abominations."
>
> **Matthew 11:20-24** Then He began to rebuke the cities in which most of His mighty works had been done, because they did not repent: "Woe to you, Chorazin! Woe to you, Bethsaida! For if the mighty works which were done in you had been done in Tyre and Sidon, they would have repented long ago in sackcloth and ashes. But I say to you, it will be more tolerable for Tyre and Sidon in the day of judgment than for you. And you, Capernaum, who are exalted to heaven, will be brought down to Hades; for if the mighty

works which were done in you had been done in Sodom, it would have remained until this day. But I say to you that it shall be more tolerable for the land of Sodom in the day of judgment than for you."

John 19:11 Jesus answered, "You could have no power at all against Me unless it had been given you from above. Therefore the one who delivered Me to you has the greater sin."

QUESTION 84

ORIGINAL

Q. 84. What doth every sin deserve?

A. Every sin deserveth God's wrath and curse, both in this life, and that which is to come.

MODERN

Q. 84. What does every sin deserve?

A. Every sin deserves God's anger and curse—not only in this life, but forever.

> **PROOF TEXTS**
>
> **Ephesians 5:6** Let no one deceive you with empty words, for because of these things the wrath of God comes upon the sons of disobedience.
>
> **Galatians 3:10** For as many as are of the works of the law are under the curse; for it is written, "Cursed is everyone who does not continue in all things which are written in the book of the law, to do them."
>
> **James 2:10** For whoever shall keep the whole law, and yet stumble in one point, he is guilty of all.
>
> **Matthew 25:41** Then He will also say to those on the left hand, 'Depart from Me, you cursed, into the everlasting fire prepared for the devil and his angels.'

QUESTION 85

ORIGINAL

Q. 85. What doth God require of us, that we may escape his wrath and curse due to us for sin?

A. To escape the wrath and curse of God due to us for sin, God requireth of us faith in Jesus Christ, repentance unto life, with the diligent use of all the outward means whereby Christ communicateth to us the benefits of redemption.

MODERN

Q. 85. What does God require of us so that we may escape His anger and curse which we deserve for our sins?

A. In order to escape the anger and curse of God, we are required to have faith in Jesus Christ and repentance unto life. We must also diligently apply the things which God uses to bring us redemption.

PROOF TEXTS

Mark 1:14-15 Now after John was put in prison, Jesus came to Galilee, preaching the gospel of the kingdom of God, and saying, "The time is fulfilled, and the kingdom of God is at hand. Repent, and believe in the gospel."

Acts 20:21 testifying to Jews, and also to Greeks, repentance toward God and faith toward our Lord Jesus Christ.

QUESTION 86

ORIGINAL

Q. 86. What is faith in Jesus Christ?

A. Faith in Jesus Christ is a saving grace, whereby we receive and rest upon him alone for salvation, as he is offered to us in the gospel.

MODERN

Q. 86. What is faith in Jesus Christ?

A. Faith in Jesus Christ is a merciful gift of God for our salvation. We have faith when we accept Christ and depend on Him alone for salvation as He is presented to us in the gospel.

PROOF TEXTS
Acts 2:38 Then Peter said to them, "Repent, and let every one of you be baptized in the name of Jesus Christ for the remission of sins; and you shall receive the gift of the Holy Spirit."
John 1:12 But as many as received Him, to them He gave the right to become children of God, to those who believe in His name
Galatians 2:16 knowing that a man is not justified by the works of the law but by faith in Jesus Christ, even we have believed in Christ Jesus, that we might be justified by faith in Christ and not by the works of the law; for by the works of the law no flesh shall be justified.

QUESTION 87

ORIGINAL

Q. 87. What is repentance unto life?

A. Repentance unto life is a saving grace, whereby a sinner, out of a true sense of his sin, and apprehension of the mercy of God in Christ, doth, with grief and hatred of his sin, turn from it unto God, with full purpose of, and endeavour after, new obedience.

MODERN

Q. 87. What is repentance unto life?

A. Repentance unto life is a merciful gift of God for our salvation. Through repentance, a sinner—having a real awareness of his sin and an understanding of the mercy of God in Christ—turns away from sin and toward God. The sinner repents with real grief and hatred of his sin, demonstrating a sincere effort to obey God.

PROOF TEXTS

Acts 11:18 When they heard these things they became silent; and they glorified God, saying, "Then God has also granted to the Gentiles repentance to life."

Joel 2:12 "Now, therefore," says the LORD, "Turn to Me with all your heart, with fasting, with weeping, and with mourning."

Isaiah 1:16-17 Wash yourselves, make yourselves clean; put away the evil of your doings from before My eyes. Cease to do evil, learn to do good; seek justice, rebuke the oppressor; defend the fatherless, plead for the widow.

QUESTION 88

ORIGINAL

Q. 88. What are the outward means whereby Christ communicateth to us the benefits of redemption?

A. The outward and ordinary means whereby Christ communicateth to us the benefits of redemption, are his ordinances, especially the Word, sacraments, and prayer; all which are made effectual to the elect for salvation.

MODERN

Q. 88. What are the outward ways in which Christ brings us the benefits of redemption?

A. The outward, ordinary ways in which Christ brings us the benefits of redemption are His ordinances—especially the Word, the sacraments, and prayer. All of these have been established by God as effective methods of bringing salvation to His people.

PROOF TEXTS

Matthew 28:19-20 Go therefore and make disciples of all the nations, baptizing them in the name of the Father and of the Son and of the Holy Spirit, teaching them to observe all things that I have commanded you; and lo, I am with you always, even to the end of the age." Amen.

Acts 2:42 And they continued steadfastly in the apostles' doctrine and fellowship, in the breaking of bread, and in prayers.

QUESTION 89

ORIGINAL

Q. 89. How is the Word made effectual to salvation?

A. The Spirit of God maketh the reading, but especially the preaching of the Word, an effectual means of convincing and converting sinners, and of building them up in holiness and comfort, through faith, unto salvation.

MODERN

Q. 89. How is the Word made effective for our salvation?

A. The Spirit of God makes the reading and especially the preaching of the Word effective in convincing and changing the hearts of sinners. Through the Word, the Spirit also encourages sinners toward holiness and brings them comfort through faith, so that they may be saved.

PROOF TEXTS

Nehemiah 8:8 So they read distinctly from the book, in the Law of God; and they gave the sense, and helped them to understand the reading.

Psalm 19:8 The statutes of the Lord are right, rejoicing the heart; the commandment of the Lord is pure, enlightening the eyes.

Romans 15:4 For whatever things were written before were written for our learning, that we through the patience and comfort of the Scriptures might have hope.

II Timothy 3:15-17 and that from childhood you have known the Holy Scriptures, which are able to make you wise for salvation through faith which is in Christ Jesus. All Scripture is given by inspiration of God, and is profitable for doctrine, for reproof, for correction, for instruction in righteousness, that the man of God may be complete, thoroughly equipped for every good work.

Romans 10:14-17 How then shall they call on Him in whom they have not believed? And how shall they believe in Him of whom they have not heard? And how shall they hear without a preacher? And how shall they preach unless they are sent? As it is written: "How beautiful are the feet of those who preach the gospel of peace, who bring glad tidings of good things!" But they have not all obeyed the gospel. For Isaiah says, "LORD, who has believed our report?" So then faith comes by hearing, and hearing by the word of God.

QUESTION 90

ORIGINAL

Q. 90. How is the Word to be read and heard, that it may become effectual to salvation?

A. That the Word may become effectual to salvation, we must attend thereunto with diligence, preparation, and prayer; receive it with faith and love, lay it up in our hearts, and practice it in our lives.

MODERN

Q. 90. How should someone read and listen to the Word so that it may be effective for salvation?

A. Anyone who reads or listens to the Word must do so attentively and with proper preparation and prayer. The Word of God must be received with faith and love, contemplated carefully, and put into practice in daily life.

> **PROOF TEXTS**
>
> **I Peter 2:1-2** Therefore, laying aside all malice, all deceit, hypocrisy, envy, and all evil speaking, as newborn babes, desire the pure milk of the word, that you may grow thereby,
>
> **Hebrews 4:2** For indeed the gospel was preached to us as well as to them; but the word which they heard did not profit them, not being mixed with faith in those who heard it.
>
> **Psalm 119:11** Your word I have hidden in my heart, that I might not sin against You.
>
> **Luke 8:15** But the ones that fell on the good ground are those who, having heard the word with a noble and good heart, keep it and bear fruit with patience.

QUESTION 91

ORIGINAL

Q. 91. How do the sacraments become effectual means of salvation?

A. The sacraments become effectual means of salvation, not from any virtue in them, or in him that doth administer them; but only by the blessing of Christ, and the working of his Spirit in them that by faith receive them.

MODERN

Q. 91. How are the sacraments effective for salvation?

A. There is nothing about the ingredients of the sacraments themselves (or about the one who administers the sacraments) which makes them effective. Only the blessing of Christ and the work of the Holy Spirit in those who receive the sacraments by faith renders them effective for salvation.

PROOF TEXTS
I Peter 3:21 There is also an antitype which now saves us—baptism (not the removal of the filth of the flesh, but the answer of a good conscience toward God), through the resurrection of Jesus Christ
I Corinthians 3:6-7 I planted, Apollos watered, but God gave the increase. So then neither he who plants is anything, nor he who waters, but God who gives the increase.

QUESTION 92

ORIGINAL

Q. 92. What is a sacrament?

A. A sacrament is an holy ordinance instituted by Christ, wherein, by sensible signs, Christ, and the benefits of the new covenant, are represented, sealed, and applied to believers.

MODERN

Q. 92. What is a sacrament?

A. A sacrament is an ordinance set apart as holy by Christ. The sacraments are physical symbols by which Christ and the benefits of the new covenant are represented, guaranteed, and applied to believers.

> **PROOF TEXTS**
>
> **Genesis 17:10** This is My covenant which you shall keep, between Me and you and your descendants after you: Every male child among you shall be circumcised
>
> **Romans 4:11** And he received the sign of circumcision, a seal of the righteousness of the faith which he had while still uncircumcised, that he might be the father of all those who believe, though they are uncircumcised, that righteousness might be imputed to them also

QUESTION 93

ORIGINAL

Q. 93. Which are the sacraments of the New Testament?

A. The sacraments of the New Testament are, Baptism, and the Lord's supper.

MODERN

Q. 93. What are the sacraments of the New Testament?

A. The sacraments of the New Testament are baptism and the Lord's supper.

PROOF TEXTS
Matthew 26:26-28 And as they were eating, Jesus took bread, blessed and broke it, and gave it to the disciples and said, "Take, eat; this is My body." Then He took the cup, and gave thanks, and gave it to them, saying, "Drink from it, all of you. For this is My blood of the new covenant, which is shed for many for the remission of sins.
Matthew 28:19 Go therefore and make disciples of all the nations, baptizing them in the name of the Father and of the Son and of the Holy Spirit

QUESTION 94

ORIGINAL

Q. 94. What is baptism?

A. Baptism is a sacrament, wherein the washing with water in the name of the Father, and of the Son, and of the Holy Ghost, doth signify and seal our ingrafting into Christ, and partaking of the benefits of the covenant of grace, and our engagement to be the Lord's.

MODERN

Q. 94. What is baptism?

A. Baptism is a sacrament in which believers are washed with water in the name of the Father, the Son, and the Holy Spirit. This sacrament is a symbol and seal proclaiming that a believer is joined with Christ, shares in the promise of grace, and belongs to the Lord.

PROOF TEXTS

Romans 6:4 Therefore we were buried with Him through baptism into death, that just as Christ was raised from the dead by the glory of the Father, even so we also should walk in newness of life.

Galatians 3:27 For as many of you as were baptized into Christ have put on Christ.

QUESTION 95

ORIGINAL

Q. 95. To whom is baptism to be administered?

A. Baptism is not to be administered to any that are out of the visible church, till they profess their faith in Christ, and obedience to him; but the infants of such as are members of the visible church are to be baptized.

MODERN

Q. 95. Who should be baptized?

A. People who are not members of a church must not be baptized until they profess their faith in Christ and their obedience to Him. However, babies of church members should be baptized.

PROOF TEXTS
Acts 8:36-37 As they went down the road, they came to some water. And the eunuch said, "See, here is water. What hinders me from being baptized?" Then Philip said, "If you believe with all your heart, you may." And he answered and said, "I believe that Jesus Christ is the Son of God."
Acts 2:38-39 Then Peter said to them, "Repent, and let every one of you be baptized in the name of Jesus Christ for the remission of sins; and you shall receive the gift of the Holy Spirit. For the promise is to you and to your children, and to all who are afar off, as many as the Lord our God will call."

QUESTION 96

ORIGINAL

Q. 96. What is the Lord's supper?

A. The Lord's supper is a sacrament, wherein, by giving and receiving bread and wine, according to Christ's appointment, his death is showed forth; and the worthy receivers are, not after a corporal and carnal manner, but by faith, made partakers of his body and blood, with all his benefits, to their spiritual nourishment, and growth in grace.

MODERN

Q. 96. What is the Lord's supper?

A. The Lord's supper is a sacrament in which bread and wine are given and received as commanded by Christ. Through this sacrament, Christ's death is declared to all. Those who participate properly in the Lord's supper receive His body and blood (not in a physical sense, but by faith) and all His blessings. They are spiritually nourished and grow in grace.

PROOF TEXTS
I Corinthians 11:23-26 For I received from the Lord that which I also delivered to you: that the Lord Jesus on the same night in which He was betrayed took bread; and when He had given thanks, He broke it and said, "Take, eat; this is My body which is broken for you; do this in remembrance of Me." In the same manner He also took the cup after supper,

saying, "This cup is the new covenant in My blood. This do, as often as you drink it, in remembrance of Me." For as often as you eat this bread and drink this cup, you proclaim the Lord's death till He comes.

I Corinthians 10:16 The cup of blessing which we bless, is it not the communion of the blood of Christ? The bread which we break, is it not the communion of the body of Christ?

QUESTION 97

ORIGINAL

Q. 97. What is required to the worthy receiving of the Lord's supper?

A. It is required of them that would worthily partake of the Lord's supper, that they examine themselves of their knowledge to discern the Lord's body, of their faith to feed upon him, of their repentance, love, and new obedience; lest, coming unworthily, they eat and drink judgment to themselves.

MODERN

Q. 97. What is required of us so that we may properly receive the Lord's supper?

A. In order to participate properly in the Lord's supper, we are required to examine our hearts in regard to our understanding of the supper as the Lord's body and our faith to feed upon Him. We should consider our repentance, love, and obedience to God. If we share in the Lord's supper improperly, we will eat and drink judgment on ourselves.

> **PROOF TEXTS**
>
> **I Corinthians 11:28-29** But let a man examine himself, and so let him eat of the bread and drink of the cup. For he who eats and drinks in an unworthy manner eats and drinks judgment to himself, not discerning the Lord's body.

II Corinthians 13:5 Examine yourselves as to whether you are in the faith. Test yourselves. Do you not know yourselves, that Jesus Christ is in you?— unless indeed you are disqualified.

I Corinthians 5:7-8 Therefore purge out the old leaven, that you may be a new lump, since you truly are unleavened. For indeed Christ, our Passover, was sacrificed for us. Therefore let us keep the feast, not with old leaven, nor with the leaven of malice and wickedness, but with the unleavened bread of sincerity and truth.

QUESTION 98

ORIGINAL

Q. 98. What is prayer?

A. Prayer is an offering up of our desires unto God for things agreeable to his will, in the name of Christ, with confession of our sins, and thankful acknowledgment of his mercies.

MODERN

Q. 98. What is prayer?

A. When we pray, we offer our requests to God for everything that is according to His plan. We confess our sins and thank God for His mercy to us. We pray always in the name of Christ.

> **PROOF TEXTS**
>
> **Psalm 62:8** Trust in Him at all times, you people; pour out your heart before Him; God is a refuge for us. Selah
>
> **I John 5:14** Now this is the confidence that we have in Him, that if we ask anything according to His will, He hears us.
>
> **Psalm 32:5-6** I acknowledged my sin to You, and my iniquity I have not hidden. I said, "I will confess my transgressions to the LORD," and You forgave the iniquity of my sin. Selah
>   For this cause everyone who is godly shall pray to You in a time when You may be found; surely in a flood of great waters they shall not come near him.
>
> **Philippians 4:6** Be anxious for nothing, but in everything by prayer and supplication, with thanksgiving, let your requests be made known to God

QUESTION 99

ORIGINAL

Q. 99. What rule hath God given for our direction in prayer?

A. The whole Word of God is of use to direct us in prayer; but the special rule of direction is that form of prayer which Christ taught his disciples, commonly called *The Lord's Prayer*.

MODERN

Q. 99. What instruction has God given to us about prayer?

A. The entire Word of God instructs us about prayer, but especially the form of prayer which Christ taught His disciples—the Lord's Prayer.

PROOF TEXTS

I John 5:14 Now this is the confidence that we have in Him, that if we ask anything according to His will, He hears us.

Matthew 6:9-13 In this manner, therefore, pray: Our Father in heaven, hallowed be Your name. Your kingdom come. Your will be done on earth as it is in heaven. Give us this day our daily bread. And forgive us our debts, as we forgive our debtors. And do not lead us into temptation, but deliver us from the evil one. For Yours is the kingdom and the power and the glory forever. Amen.

QUESTION 100

ORIGINAL

Q. 100. What doth the preface of the Lord's prayer teach us?

A. The preface of the Lord's prayer (which is, Our Father which art in heaven) teacheth us to draw near to God with all holy reverence and confidence, as children to a father, able and ready to help us; and that we should pray with and for others.

MODERN

Q. 100. What does the introduction of the Lord's Prayer teach us?

A. The introduction of the Lord's Prayer (*Our Father in heaven*) teaches us to approach God with holy reverence and confidence, like children approach their father. We should believe that God is able and ready to help us. We should include other people in our prayers—both praying with them and for them.

PROOF TEXTS

Matthew 6:9 In this manner, therefore, pray: Our Father in heaven, hallowed be Your name.

Romans 8:15 For you did not receive the spirit of bondage again to fear, but you received the Spirit of adoption by whom we cry out, "Abba, Father."

Ephesians 6:18 praying always with all prayer and supplication in the Spirit, being watchful to this end with all perseverance and supplication for all the saints—

QUESTION 101

ORIGINAL

Q. 101. What do we pray for in the first petition?

A. In the first petition (which is, Hallowed be thy name,) we pray, That God would enable us and others to glorify him in all that whereby he maketh himself known; and that he would dispose all things to his own glory.

MODERN

Q. 101. What do we pray for in the first request?

A. In the first request (*Hallowed be Your name*), we pray that God would enable us and others to honor Him in everything by which He makes Himself known. We also pray that He would use all things for His glory.

> **PROOF TEXTS**
>
> **Matthew 6:9** In this manner, therefore, pray: Our Father in heaven, hallowed be Your name.
>
> **Psalm 67:1-3** God be merciful to us and bless us, and cause His face to shine upon us, Selah
>   That Your way may be known on earth, Your salvation among all nations. Let the peoples praise You, O God; let all the peoples praise You.

QUESTION 102

ORIGINAL

Q. 102. What do we pray for in the second petition?

A. In the second petition (which is, Thy kingdom come,) we pray, That Satan's kingdom may be destroyed; and that the kingdom of grace may be advanced, ourselves and others brought into it, and kept in it; and that the kingdom of glory may be hastened.

MODERN

Q. 102. What do we pray for in the second request?

A. In the second request (*Your kingdom come*), we pray that Satan's kingdom would be destroyed. We pray that the kingdom of grace would press forward and that many (including ourselves) would be brought into it and kept in it. We also pray that the glorious kingdom of God would come quickly.

PROOF TEXTS
Matthew 6:10 Your kingdom come. Your will be done on earth as it is in heaven.
Psalm 68:1 Let God arise, let His enemies be scattered; let those also who hate Him flee before Him.
II Thessalonians 3:1 Finally, brethren, pray for us, that the word of the Lord may run swiftly and be glorified, just as it is with you

Revelation 12:10-11 Then I heard a loud voice saying in heaven, "Now salvation, and strength, and the kingdom of our God, and the power of His Christ have come, for the accuser of our brethren, who accused them before our God day and night, has been cast down. And they overcame him by the blood of the Lamb and by the word of their testimony, and they did not love their lives to the death.

Romans 10:1 Brethren, my heart's desire and prayer to God for Israel is that they may be saved.

John 17:20 I do not pray for these alone, but also for those who will believe in Me through their word

Revelation 22:20 He who testifies to these things says, "Surely I am coming quickly." Amen. Even so, come, Lord Jesus!

QUESTION 103

ORIGINAL

Q. 103. What do we pray for in the third petition?

A. In the third petition (which is, Thy will be done in earth, as it is in heaven,) we pray, That God, by his grace, would make us able and willing to know, obey, and submit to his will in all things, as the angels do in heaven.

MODERN

Q. 103. What do we pray for in the third request?

A. In the third request (*Your will be done on earth as it is in heaven*), we pray that God would graciously enable us to know, obey, and submit to His will in everything, like the angels in heaven know and obey Him.

> **PROOF TEXTS**
>
> **Matthew 6:10** Your kingdom come. Your will be done on earth as it is in heaven.
>
> **Psalm 119:34-36** Give me understanding, and I shall keep Your law; indeed, I shall observe it with my whole heart. Make me walk in the path of Your commandments, for I delight in it. Incline my heart to Your testimonies, and not to covetousness.
>
> **Acts 21:14** So when he would not be persuaded, we ceased, saying, "The will of the Lord be done."
>
> **Job 1:21** And he said: "Naked I came from my mother's womb, and naked shall I return there. The LORD gave, and the LORD has taken away; blessed be the name of the LORD."

Matthew 26:39 He went a little farther and fell on His face, and prayed, saying, "O My Father, if it is possible, let this cup pass from Me; nevertheless, not as I will, but as You will."

Psalm 103:20-21 Bless the LORD, you His angels, who excel in strength, who do His word, heeding the voice of His word. Bless the LORD, all you His hosts, you ministers of His, who do His pleasure.

QUESTION 104

ORIGINAL

Q. 104. What do we pray for in the fourth petition?

A. In the fourth petition (which is, Give us this day our daily bread,) we pray, That of God's free gift we may receive a competent portion of the good things of this life, and enjoy his blessing with them.

MODERN

Q. 104. What do we pray for in the fourth request?

A. In the fourth request (*Give us this day our daily bread*), we pray that God would freely provide us with a sufficient supply of the good things of life and that we may enjoy His blessing.

> **PROOF TEXTS**
>
> **Matthew 6:11** Give us this day our daily bread.
>
> **Proverbs 30:8-9** Remove falsehood and lies far from me; give me neither poverty nor riches—feed me with the food allotted to me; lest I be full and deny You, and say, "Who is the LORD?" or lest I be poor and steal, and profane the name of my God.
>
> **Psalm 90:17** And let the beauty of the LORD our God be upon us, and establish the work of our hands for us; yes, establish the work of our hands.

QUESTION 105

ORIGINAL

Q. 105. What do we pray for in the fifth petition?

A. In the fifth petition (which is, And forgive us our debts, as we forgive our debtors,) we pray, That God, for Christ's sake, would freely pardon all our sins; which we are the rather encouraged to ask, because by his grace we are enabled from the heart to forgive others.

MODERN

Q. 105. What do we pray for in the fifth request?

A. In the fifth request (*forgive us our debts, as we forgive our debtors*), we pray that God would freely forgive all our sins for the sake of Christ. We are encouraged to ask for God's forgiveness, because His grace enables us to sincerely forgive others.

PROOF TEXTS

Matthew 6:12 And forgive us our debts, as we forgive our debtors.

Psalm 51:1-2 Have mercy upon me, O God, according to Your lovingkindness; according to the multitude of Your tender mercies, blot out my transgressions. Wash me thoroughly from my iniquity, and cleanse me from my sin.

Matthew 18:35 So My heavenly Father also will do to you if each of you, from his heart, does not forgive his brother his trespasses.

Daniel 9:17-19 Now therefore, our God, hear the prayer of Your servant, and his supplications, and for the Lord's sake cause Your face to shine on Your sanctuary, which is desolate. O my God, incline Your ear and hear; open Your eyes and see our desolations, and the city which is called by Your name; for we do not present our supplications before You because of our righteous deeds, but because of Your great mercies. O Lord, hear! O Lord, forgive! O Lord, listen and act! Do not delay for Your own sake, my God, for Your city and Your people are called by Your name.

QUESTION 106

ORIGINAL

Q. 106. What do we pray for in the sixth petition?

A. In the sixth petition (which is, And lead us not into temptation, but deliver us from evil,) we pray, That God would either keep us from being tempted to sin, or support and deliver us when we are tempted.

MODERN

Q. 106. What do we pray for in the sixth request?

A. In the sixth request (*do not lead us into temptation, but deliver us from evil*), we pray that God would either prevent temptation to sin or that He would support us and deliver us when we are tempted to sin.

> **PROOF TEXTS**
>
> **Matthew 6:13** And do not lead us into temptation, but deliver us from the evil one. For Yours is the kingdom and the power and the glory forever. Amen.
>
> **Psalm 19:13** Keep back Your servant also from presumptuous sins; let them not have dominion over me. Then I shall be blameless, and I shall be innocent of great transgression.
>
> **II Corinthians 12:7-8** And lest I should be exalted above measure by the abundance of the revelations, a thorn in the flesh was given to me, a messenger of Satan to buffet me, lest I be exalted above measure. Concerning this thing I pleaded with the Lord three times that it might depart from me.

QUESTION 107

ORIGINAL

Q. 107. What doth the conclusion of the Lord's prayer teach us?

A. The conclusion of the Lord's prayer (which is, For thine is the kingdom, and the power, and the glory, for ever, Amen.) teacheth us, to take our encouragement in prayer from God only, and in our prayers to praise him, ascribing kingdom, power, and glory to him. And, in testimony of our desire, and assurance to be heard, we say, Amen.

MODERN

Q. 107. What does the conclusion of the Lord's Prayer teach us?

A. The conclusion of the Lord's Prayer (*For Yours is the kingdom and the power and the glory forever. Amen.*) teaches us that our encouragement in prayer should only be found in God, and that we should praise Him and acknowledge His kingdom, power, and glory. To demonstrate that we want to be heard and that we know God hears us, we say, "Amen."

PROOF TEXTS

Daniel 9:18-19 O my God, incline Your ear and hear; open Your eyes and see our desolations, and the city which is called by Your name; for we do not present our supplications before You because of our righteous deeds, but because of Your great mercies. O Lord, hear! O Lord, forgive! O Lord, listen and act! Do not delay for Your own sake, my God, for Your city and Your people are called by Your name.

I Chronicles 29:10-13 Therefore David blessed the Lord before all the assembly; and David said: "Blessed are You, Lord God of Israel, our Father, forever and ever. Yours, O Lord, is the greatness, the power and the glory, the victory and the majesty; for all that is in heaven and in earth is Yours; Yours is the kingdom, O Lord, and You are exalted as head over all. Both riches and honor come from You, and You reign over all. In Your hand is power and might; in Your hand it is to make great and to give strength to all. Now therefore, our God, we thank You and praise Your glorious name."

Revelation 22:20-21 He who testifies to these things says, "Surely I am coming quickly." Amen. Even so, come, Lord Jesus! The grace of our Lord Jesus Christ be with you all. Amen.

Made in the USA
Charleston, SC
19 May 2012